RETAIL PRIDE

Megan—
Keep your retail
pride strong!

Ron

RETAIL

PRIDE

THE GUIDE TO
CELEBRATING
YOUR ACCIDENTAL
CAREER

RON
THURSTON

LIONCREST
PUBLISHING

RETAIL PRIDE
The Guide to Celebrating Your Accidental Career

ISBN   978-1-5445-1593-9 *Hardcover*
       978-1-5445-1592-2 *Paperback*
       978-1-5445-1591-5 *Ebook*

For my grandfather, Oscar Faoro
(1919–2012)

Oscar showed me how to be a leader,
a husband, and a teacher.

More than anyone I have known, he
proved to me that people could overcome
the limits put on themselves, and it's our
responsibility to discover their light.

He taught me that if you do everything
with integrity and pride, your most
significant impact will be ahead of you,
and you might not even know it.

I love you, Papa.

WITH CONTRIBUTIONS FROM

Anthony Pierce

Brandon Lee

Christine Wertman

Dameron Fooks

Dana Perez-Elhai

Doug Riccio

Elizabeth (EK)
  Korczykowski

Gail Topal

Garth W. Jackson

Jenny Aguon

Jill Grande

Jin Hur

Kemoy Duhaney

Kim Even

Kristin Smith

Leandra Reid

Lisa Molinari

Orlando Roble

Patricia Elmaleh

Rick Planos

Roy McCombs

Saira Sethi

Shannon Smith

Steve Hawkins

Steve Yacker

Tod Hallman

Tori Keller

Tracy Heureux

Walt Holbrook

William Brobston

CONTENTS

THERE IS A SPECIAL LIGHT THAT SHINES BRIGHTER IN RETAIL PEOPLE. WE HAVE A NATURAL SENSE OF POSITIVITY, A CONSTANT DRIVE TO IMPROVE, TO DELIVER THE BEST RESULTS, TO HUSTLE, TO CONNECT.

INTRODUCTION

Everyone. Everywhere. Every day.

That's how big this is. Everyone in the world is impacted by retail. Every day. When I think about the size, scale, and positive influence of this industry, it gives me great joy, because I know there are millions of people who love working in retail, and they need to be celebrated.

Retail is woven into every city in the country. It's where most teenagers get their first job. It's where friends meet to hang out, and it's the industry that comes together most often when communities face a natural disaster, need a donation drive, or see an opportunity to raise money for a cause.

Small businesses, especially retail stores, often contribute to the heart of a community where business associations and local government work collectively to preserve the character of their town. As advocates for the industry, we have an unparalleled ability to create compelling, positive, economic impact and rally our teams around causes.

I was finishing the final version of this manuscript when COVID-19 caused the most significant economic shift that we have ever experienced. As a retail industry, we now have the platform, the resources, the necessity, and the people to reconnect the world. *Our sector will be forever altered, but we now have a responsibility to each other and our customers to be our best and connect more deeply than we have ever needed to before.*

I have both the experience to write about the state of the retail industry and a story to tell. A good story. A story that people will want to talk about. Perhaps it has something in common with your story. Millions of people work in retail. The majority of us work in stores, and our stories need to be told.

If you work in retail at any level, I wrote this book for you. It's for all employees, teams, and leaders. The voice you'll hear in these pages is my voice, the voice of someone who has done the work, and lived through the joy and the pain. What you won't find is corporate jargon about "leadership" that doesn't apply to retail. We speak the same language; we understand each other's energy and drive. If there were a secret handshake for people who work in stores, I would have invented it.

There is a special light that shines brighter in retail people. We have a natural sense of positivity, a constant drive to improve, to deliver the best results, to hustle, to connect. And nobody loves contests more than we do. We can't wait for conferences, celebrations, high fives, awards, and goofy posters in the stockroom.

But here is the reality; many of us didn't imagine we'd work in retail. You may have started working just to make some extra money or gain some general experience. You didn't study "retail leadership" in college. You stuck with it when you realized how much you loved it, even though some of your friends and family said you could do something else. Sure, you might be able to make more money in a different industry, but you are doing what you're good at. You're doing what you love.

If you've ever said, "I work in retail" and not felt proud of those words, this book is for you. If you've ever beamed with pride at earning a promotion and receiving the keys to your store, this book is for you. If you've ever dealt with friends and family asking you when you'll get a real job, this book is for you.

This book is for anyone who found their way into retail and is now fully committed to this exciting career.

This accidental career.

This is my story. This is your story. This is our retail story.

MY STORY

How many times in a month are you asked the question, *"So what do you do?"*

As an executive who attends a lot of networking events, I get this question quite often. I used to dread the question because I wasn't sure how to answer it. I would respond, "I work in retail." I wanted to be true to myself, but I didn't want to sound like my career was an accident or unimportant.

Now, I *love* answering that question! I've found a way to describe my retail career that fills me with pride and meaning.

No matter how many different jobs or work experiences you've had, nor how disparate they may seem, there is one thread that usually ties them together. Whether you realize it or not, you have a consistent motivation for choosing the work you do. For me, that common thread has been service. First, in a traditional customer-facing role, and now through serving my teams and digging deeply into what excellent service really means. I have always loved helping people discover their potential and find their light.

How do I describe my career now? I'm glad you asked.

I lead retail teams to discover their highest potential with my empathy, curiosity, and focus on winning. And I'm proud of it.

I lead retail teams to discover their highest potential with my empathy, curiosity, and focus on winning. And I'm proud of it.

I grew up in South Lake Tahoe, California, the first child of my parents and the first grandchild in a family of fourth-generation Californians. The pressure to fulfill my destiny as the first-born son and become a successful man was part of my life from a very young age. I still feel that pressure today.

South Lake Tahoe is an idyllic, picturesque part of the world with stunning mountains, a deep blue lake, and some of the best skiing on the West Coast. I grew up in a home hand-built by my maternal grandfather. On the outside, it was an actual log house.

In the 1970s my father was a traveling wholesale toy salesman. He was one of those people everyone liked, with a huge smile and a lot of natural charm. He could have sold anything. For my two brothers and me, the constant stream of new toys was a real bonus. In many ways, I am more similar to him than I like to admit. He had an engineering degree and an accidental career.

Ultimately, the inspiration for my career came from my maternal grandfather. His name was Oscar, which means *"God spear, or champion warrior."* Oscar was certainly a champion warrior and leader, in the best possible way. He played a significant role in creating the city of South Lake Tahoe, California, building the first firehouse and some of the original schools, retail stores, and custom homes. He started a construction company that built Safeway grocery stores, and ultimately the business became quite large. It employed most of my family in leadership roles, along with dozens of other people.

At the age of fifteen, I started spending summers with my grandfather, taking road trips to Safeway construction sites all across the West Coast and observing him in action. I remember arriving on the job site and watching him make an immediate positive impact, something I aspire to emulate to this day whenever I arrive on a store visit today. I was fascinated by the way he interacted with everyone around him. He knew essential details about everyone on the job, not only their names but things about their family. He asked personal questions that were unique and relevant. A lot of handshakes, a lot of hugs. Sometimes tears.

These people were proud to work for him, and I will never forget how it made me feel seeing their reaction to Oscar. He knew how to create an employee experience that built loyalty, a concept I'll discuss later in the book. *In every business, leadership is about people, and Oscar made connecting look effortless.* It's a skill I learned from him. Whenever anyone asked Oscar how he was doing, he would say, "I couldn't be better!" Those men and women would have done anything for Oscar, and he would have done anything for them.

I attended a public high school in the suburbs of Sacramento, California. Among my peers, the typical career paths were law, medicine, and getting a corporate job. I listened to other people's ideas about what they were going to do, but no one seemed to have the career I wanted. I knew I was going to create my own story; I just didn't know what it was.

As I contemplated my career path, my grandfather was a huge influence. At the same time, with the support of my grandmother, I was discovering my love of design, garment construction, and fashion history. She owned a fabric store in South Lake Tahoe and taught me how to sew. The prospect of working for my grandfather in the family construction business—and possibly rising to an executive position—was intriguing. But I knew I had a purpose that somehow involved the fashion design and retail industry. And Oscar would be my mentor in leadership and life for decades to come.

After graduating from the Fashion Institute of Design and Merchandising (FIDM) twice with degrees in Retail Management and Fashion Design, a nod to both my grandparents, I understood both the business of retail and the art of design. I landed a job working as a patternmaker, which evolved into an Assistant Designer role, and ultimately, I became a decent fashion designer. I gained some industry recognition, and things were moving in the right direction.

But I knew I wanted more. In my late twenties, I took a 180-degree turn and used my second degree from FIDM to join the Macy's Department Store Management Training Program. I took a significant pay cut, but I was ready to start over. Spending that year in the exciting world of retail as a department manager helped me understand what I wanted more profoundly than I ever had before. I discovered a clear purpose. I found my passion. I found my tribe in retail.

I was hungry to make my mark, and for the last twenty-five years, I have been lucky enough to work with some of the most influential brands in retail history, including GAP, Apple, Tory Burch, Bonobos, Saint Laurent, and INTERMIX. In choosing which companies to work for, I've thought less about the products sold and more about each company's importance to our culture. I have held every position and grown through the ranks from part-time sales to Vice President of Stores.

It has been a career of hard work, sweat, patience, determination, and love. I have had great success and significant failures. I have known emotional highs and lows, neither of which I will ever forget.

I thrive when I see the hunger and excitement I felt in those days in the eyes of new retail leaders I meet today. They want to take on the world and show everyone what they can do. They want to control every aspect of their store, deliver exceptional results, build a strong team, and make their store a fantastic place to shop and work. The love of the retail industry spans generations.

It has been a career of hard work, sweat, patience, determination, and love. I have had great success and significant failures. I have known emotional highs and lows, neither of which I will ever forget.

Looking back at everything I've built, I'm proud of my retail career. I recognize that now. If someone tells you that retail is an accidental career unworthy of the recognition accorded to other professions, ignore them. *We make a positive impact on the lives of millions. We bring people together in tightly knit communities all across the country. We teach emotional learning skills and meet some of the most fundamental human needs.*

I can't wait for the next time someone asks me what I do.

WHAT TO EXPECT FROM THIS BOOK

This book is a manifesto. I've spilled everything I have learned onto the pages. If you've ever felt hesitant about revealing your retail career to people you meet, as I used to, I want you to know that you're not alone and don't need to feel that way. Retail matters.

The first part of this book is dedicated to a discussion about the changing landscape and the reasons why we love retail. In a post-COVID-19 world, many aspects of the business will change, some immediately, others in the long term.

By the time you finish reading, I want you to feel proud that you have chosen a career in retail, or that one chose you. I want you to feel as prepared as possible for the many challenges you'll face in a rapidly evolving industry. For that reason, the second part of the book is dedicated to the primary pillars of retail expertise—skills that you need no matter what role you play in a retail environment. Each skill is followed by a section on "How to put it to work."

For the leaders and aspiring leaders among you, the third part is packed with foundational skills you will need to master to succeed. The fourth and final part of the book is the icing on the cake. It's a discussion of the character traits and advanced skills that will allow you to truly shine in a retail environment.

In case you need further inspiration, interspersed among the text of this book are quotes from thirty of my friends and colleagues who have generously shared their stories and wisdom. I also share many of my own observations about my career and the best practices that have shaped my own story.

I hope you enjoy the journey and emerge on the other side with a newfound respect for the career you've made your own, the skills that enable you to succeed in your role, and the difference you make in the lives of others.

PART I

FINDING THAT BALANCE BETWEEN REMEMBERING THE PAST AND INVESTING IN NEW IDEAS IS ESSENTIAL TO OUR FUTURE.

CHAPTER 1

REDEFINING RETAIL FOR A NEW WORLD

It's no secret that the retail landscape is more competitive today than ever before. And the speed and complexity of the changing economy are not going to diminish. *There has never been a more significant time to work in retail, to love what you do, and to be better at it than you ever have before.*

I am not going to try to predict the future in this book. The intent here is to celebrate the millions of men and women who work in retail, not to share my thoughts on new store concepts. The principles of good retail were the same a hundred years ago as they are today. But that doesn't mean we should not be acutely aware of what is happening around us or how we need to evolve as an industry.

The key to navigating this new paradigm shift is to balance the past with new innovative ideas. I love to study retail history; understanding retail principles that have always been the same gives me perspective on what is unique about our current circumstances. We need to evolve along with our customers while still remembering the fundamentals of our business. *Finding that balance between remembering the past and investing in new ideas is essential to our future.*

For nearly as long as people have existed, we have been sharing, bartering, selling, and consuming resources. As far back as 9000 BC, farmers exchanged cows and sheep. By 800 BC, in ancient Greece, the first retail stores came into existence. People developed markets to sell their wares in the city center, and Greek citizens visited these markets to shop, socialize, and to participate in government.

In the eighteenth and nineteenth centuries, particularly in the late 1800s, family-run stores were plentiful throughout the United States. Many were general stores selling everything from groceries and fabrics to toys and tools.

As a little boy from Northern California, I learned firsthand about the California Gold Rush in 1848. The news of gold brought approximately 300,000 people to California from all over the world, reinvigorating the state's economy. "Old Sacramento" as it's referred to, was built during that era and is still there today with wooden sidewalks, horse-drawn carriages, old-fashioned candy shops, and Mississippi-style riverboats. An authentic retail experience of a different age that is still alive today.

The pioneering spirit of people moving west supported the evolution of shopping into the twentieth century. Industries like oil, steel, textiles, and food production grew, and factories brought new jobs and higher living standards. Department stores like Macy's (1858), Bloomingdales (1861), and Sears (1886) began popping up in cities like New York City and Chicago.

These stores didn't just sell the necessities. They also hosted demonstrations, lectures, and entertainment events that appealed to newly wealthy customers looking to spend their disposable income. One hundred fifty years later, people are still looking for exciting content and personal experiences to be of their shopping activities, and brands are finding success in all kinds of fascinating formats. New concepts like "showrooming," direct-to-consumer pop-ups, and Instagram have all changed the game.

Spring of 2020 marked a new chapter in retail history. The spread of COVID-19 has heralded a profound shift in consumer behavior, requiring all retailers to look through a wider lens and develop more innovative e-commerce and in-store experiences.

There are numerous ways to provide a personal touch for e-commerce customers; options to customize products are very popular. Personalized digital fit guides can be crowd pleasers, as they allow customers to see the product on body types like theirs in a virtual fitting room experience. You can also visit a website and receive style tips from algorithms based on your in-store purchase history, online behavior, and social media interactions.

But with the growth of the e-commerce business and the necessity of online shopping, it's increasingly evident that this segment of the industry is about to go through a major identity crisis. Customers are overwhelmed by the number of choices available online and crave the personal attention and curated selection that only a brick-and-mortar store can provide. This is our opportunity to shine. Now is the time to be our best, and to highlight the vital role our industry plays in the global economy.

Digital experiences will never replace your relationship with the person at your local store who knows you best. *Nothing is more personalized than your communication with an exceptional, curious, empathetic, and focused sales associate, who educates, comforts, and encourages you.*

So how many customers are still shopping in stores? The data is surprising and often misunderstood. While the news may be full of store closures, customer shopping habits reveal that people still crave the in-store experience.

LET'S GET A FEW FACTS STRAIGHT

Even as the retail world evolves at a breakneck pace, it's essential to understand its size and relevance. Statistics matter because they help us put our experiences into perspective. As we enter a new era of history and think about the future, let's explore the facts.

FACT #1: THE RETAIL INDUSTRY IS THE BIGGEST EMPLOYER IN THE US

Whether or not we realize it, most Americans spend a significant amount of time shopping. On average, we spend nearly forty-five minutes a day (more than 270 hours per year) purchasing goods and services.[1] We

---

1   "American Time Use Survey: 2019 Results," U.S. Bureau of Labor Statistics, June 25, 2020.

shop through a variety of channels, including brick-and-mortar retail, e-commerce, and social media.

Walk into any store, and you may be met by a greeter supplementing their income in retirement, assisted by a salesperson with a college degree, checked-out by a cashier who is a single parent, and have your purchases carried to your car by a college student working to pay tuition. In the store, you may see a leader like yourself who has been with the company for years and worked her way up from being a cashier, or you may see someone unloading a truck as his second job. Our interactions with the retail sector may fly under the radar, but they are nonetheless occurring.

According to the latest data from the National Retail Federation in March of 2020, retail provides 42 million American jobs. The industry is the largest private-sector employer in the United States, providing one in four jobs.[2]

There are 3.6 million retail establishments in the United States, collectively generating $2.6 trillion in annual GDP.[3] To be fair, the term "retail establishment" refers to everything from convenience stores, to your

---

2   "Retail supports 42 million American jobs," National Retail Federation, accessed August 26, 2020

3   "The Economic Impact of the U.S. Retail Industry," National Retail Federation, accessed August 26, 2020.

local Target, grocery stores, to luxury specialty boutiques. Nonetheless, we work in the most significant industry in the country. Be proud of that.

FACT #2: MOST SALES ARE STILL MADE IN STORES

Modern retail is indisputably a combination of physical and digital commerce. Nearly all of the top fifty online brands maintain physical stores, and 84 percent of US commerce occurred offline in 2019.[4] With intermingled inventories, shared customer audiences, and interdependent strategies, online interactions influence physical store visits just as in-store engagements may fuel digital purchases.

In the late 1990s, the e-commerce business made up less than 5 percent of total retail sales. By 2019, that figure had grown to around 12 percent. This number will continue to grow but will never completely tip the balance in favor of e-commerce and away from sales made in brick-and-mortar stores.[5]

After World War II, the economy heated up, and people left the big cities to buy new homes in the suburbs. Developers quickly followed, opening up new malls every year across

---

4   "State of Retail," National Retail Federation, accessed August 26, 2020.
5   Kate Rooney, "Online shopping overtakes a major part of retail for the first time ever," CNBC, April 3, 2019.

the country. In 1990 alone, nineteen major modern malls opened in the United States. Fast forward to today, and much of that expansive development is reversing as the way we shop evolves and brands assess how many stores they should maintain for optimal profitability, customer count growth, and brand awareness.

How your customers buy and where they receive your products can't take precedence over giving them the best possible experience.

The reality is that many stores are closing for the same reason they've always closed; they no longer meet the customers' needs. I am not going to try to predict the number of store closures, but don't let the headlines fool you. Analysts say the industry was due for trimming after decades-long mall booms and years of excessive store count expansion.

All of this is to say that how your customers buy and where they receive your products can't take precedence over giving them the best possible experience—and stores have a natural advantage in creating an experience that is memorable, powerful, and even life-changing.

FACT #3: RETAIL IS WHERE MANY AMERICANS GET THEIR FIRST JOB

I have heard it said many times that everyone needs to work in a service position at least once in their lives.

I couldn't agree more. Aside from the experience I gained observing my grandfather, I got my first real job at the age of eighteen, while I was in college. The role was selling men's luxury suits in a department store, the Broadway, in downtown San Francisco. I remember it well because I had no idea what I was doing, but I still consider it one of the best jobs I have ever had.

Why? It taught me the value of serving others, just as I had observed my grandfather serving others when he worked with his teams on a construction site. Throughout my career, I followed three primary pillars of retail expertise that I'll discuss in-depth later: empathy, curiosity, and focus. Ultimately, those three qualities started me on the journey that led me to write this book.

To give you an idea of how vital the industry is to employment in America, here are some facts:

- Thirty-two percent of all first jobs are in retail, at the average age of sixteen.
- Today, one in four American teenagers works in retail.
- Six in ten Americans have worked a retail job.[6]

---

6   "Retail supports 42 million American jobs."

Starting in those first retail jobs, we develop skills like keeping our composure, maintaining boundaries, and coping with the pressure of hitting a goal. From first jobs to lifelong careers, retail launches more people into employment than any other industry. *From the part-time sales associate at a local store on Main Street to an app developer for a major company, the industry is in every city in the country, every day.*

In 2019, a National Retail Federation study found that hiring managers across industries believe retail work experience develops the skills and traits they seek in prospective job candidates.[7] In the same survey, the majority of hiring managers recommended that applicants put this experience on their resumes, noting that retail provides foundational skills that are transferable to other industries.

Bottom line, this industry is a *great* place to learn essential skills that can put you in a good position as your career progresses—whether to a higher-level store position or another industry.

---

7   "Retail's Value on a Resume: How jobs in retail prepare America's workforce for success," National Retail Federation, June 2, 2015.

FACT #4: SHOPPING THERAPY IS REAL, AS WE DISCOVERED IN 2020

Remember the saying, "When the going gets tough, the tough go shopping?" Ask any of your friends who love to shop, and they will tell you that retail therapy is real, and that shopping can make you happier. While "therapy" isn't quite the word I would use to describe the positive effects of shopping, there are indeed psychological rewards.

This temporary boost might also have something to do with the fact that shopping gives us a perception of control, as we regulate what we take into our lives. Besides, shopping is a social activity—whether we do it with friends or simply enjoy getting out of the house and connecting with other people.

We all discovered how real that is in the spring of 2020 when in addition to not being able to see family and friends in person, we lost the connection to others that retail provides. *As we become more technologically entrenched, we will all crave better physical store experiences.*

> **As we become more technologically entrenched, we will all crave better physical store experiences.**

Does shopping online offer comparable benefits? Maybe not. Going to a store for many customers is more convenient than ordering, waiting, finally trying on an item, and then—surprise!—discovering that it doesn't fit. There's nothing therapeutic about disappointment, followed by a wait for a refund.

Brick-and-mortar retailers also offer a variety of companies the opportunity to draw us into their story, deliver a remarkable and immersive product experience, and solidify the relationship between the customer and the brand. That relationship can then live across multiple buying channels and become a brand's most valuable asset.

THE MORE THINGS CHANGE

We live in a time of enormous change. Even before COVID-19 hit, the industry was going through a tremendous shift. Now that dynamic has been amplified. Retail will continue to evolve and change, and no one can know what new innovations will emerge over the coming decade.

One thing we can say with confidence, however, is that it isn't disappearing anytime soon. It remains the largest employer in the country, and most sales are still made in stores despite the rise in online shopping. Retail is where millions of young Americans cut their teeth in the world of employment and learn valuable skills. Plus, shopping makes people feel good!

Despite all the changes, this is a valued industry that will remain important and continue making a vital emotional and financial contribution to the lives of millions of people.

WHAT WE DO
OR DON'T DO
ON SATURDAY
IS LIMITED
ONLY BY OUR
CREATIVITY,
THE TEAM WE
SURROUND
OURSELVES
WITH, AND
OUR DRIVE
FOR RESULTS.

CHAPTER 2

TEN REASONS TO LOVE WORKING IN RETAIL

Saturday is my favorite day at work.

Think about it for a minute. For many working people, Monday is when they get back to the workaday grind, while Friday is likely the day they look forward to most because the work week is over.

But not in retail! Saturday is when we connect the world. Saturday is the day to shake up those brain cells, bring our best energy, and have our best sales day of the week. It's the day we focus on what we love most: spending time with our team and ensuring we provide exceptional experiences at every turn, no matter our individual roles.

When I was a store manager, I rarely took a Saturday off. It was always my favorite day because the possibilities were endless. There were few tasks, no district manager bothering me (usually!), and no conference calls.

After years of working weekends, I can confidently say that what we do or don't do on Saturday is limited only by our creativity, the team we surround ourselves with, and our drive for results.

Why is this important? Because it demonstrates our love of retail. The busiest day, the day we are the most exhausted, is our favorite day. That says so much about who we are and how we think.

You understand this mindset. You recognize the satisfaction of serving people, crushing your goals, and going home at the end of the day ready to drop but incredibly fulfilled. In this chapter, I want to share my ten reasons why retail is such a unique environment, in the hope that you'll see yourself in the words, recognize how much you love your job, and stand a little bit taller the next time you work on Saturday.

REASON #1: WE CREATE JOY

Customers no longer need to go to a physical store to buy a product. As a result, the strategic purpose of the store has changed. Shopping in stores must either be as cheap and convenient as ordering from Amazon, or it must be entertaining and educational, offering memorable experiences that can't be replicated online.

It's hard to compete with Amazon on price, but we can certainly compete on joy. Whatever that might look like for your company, whatever products you sell, make that visit to your store a joyful one. "Experiential Retail" is one of the most prominent buzz phrases of the last decade, and we continue to read about how creating unique experiences is the only way we will survive. I would go further and say that if you are just now figuring this out, you're late to the conversation.

It's hard to compete with Amazon on price, but we can certainly compete on joy.

Retailers take pride in creating joy. It sits squarely as the first reason we love working in retail, because we are obsessed with creating exceptional customer experiences. *We work hard to build deep, long-lasting relationships, and we continually seek inspiration to improve.* In 1993, Ken Blanchard and Sheldon

Bowles wrote a book called Raving Fans that changed how many of us thought about service. While it was not specifically about retail, we clung onto that book as the first words about business and service that we related to.

> **We work hard to build deep, long-lasting relationships, and we continually seek inspiration to improve.**

The authors wrote: "Your customers are only satisfied because their expectations are so low and because no one else is doing better. Just having satisfied customers isn't good enough anymore. If you want a booming business, you have to create Raving Fans."

And that was in 1993!

The "Raving Fans" mentality enables a company to exceed everyone's expectations, consistently. Consistently being the key word. When you get to know your customers, lead with curiosity, integrate into their lives, evolve with them as their lives change, and find fluidity in how you serve them, the relationship gets even more profound.

When we don't deliver on the smallest expectations of the customer, what we say to them is, "we don't care if you shop here." As we race toward a world where online channels and stores share all the same customers and business opportunities, that's not an option. The future is "channel-less." The customer has choices, and human interactions and joy are at the heart of all we do.

What happens when it all works together, and you spark joy in your customers? It's magic! The customer engages with the brand on a much deeper level; they go out of their way to come and see you; they enjoy being in the store, sharing their experiences with friends and family, and spending more money.

LISA MOLINARI
Corporate Sales Manager, twenty years in retail

"I love the customer experience and the joy and excitement I see when sales associates start developing new customer connections and realize that their training and hard work has paid off."

JILL GRANDE
Senior Director, twenty-one years in retail

"My love of retail started as a young girl watching fashion shows on the Style Network. It drove me to retail as a teenager the minute I could get a work permit. Now I understand how we bring joy to thousands of strangers' lives each week, and that makes me so proud."

REASON #2: WE DON'T
GIVE UP WHEN IT'S HARD

The impact of COVID-19 on the retail industry can't be disputed. Countless jobs were lost, stores closed, entire companies shut down. But here's what I know; we will continue to find the strength to keep going and get back up on our feet. We do the work because it's important.

I saw it firsthand as I led my own retail organization in 2020. All we can do is move forward and do what we love. We keep going when others quit, and we don't give up when it's hard.

When you're pursuing a worthwhile goal, it's almost inevitable that you'll have one or more of the following thoughts:

- "This is harder than I thought it would be."
- "Why is this taking so long?"
- "I'm getting nowhere with this."
- "I keep failing at this goal."
- "I'm afraid of what's next."
- "I don't have any new ideas."

You may want to throw in the towel when any of these thoughts get in your head. *When that happens, think about how strong you are, how much you love what you* do, how hard you have worked to succeed in your accidental career, and how proud you are of your team. Even when the tables are turned against us in retail, we keep going. When those moments hit me, and they certainly do, I tell myself things like:

> **Think about how strong you are, how much you love what you do, how hard you have worked to succeed in your accidental career, and how proud you are of your team.**

- "I keep going when things get tough."
- "I'll either find a way or make one."
- "Every problem has a solution, and I can find it."
- "Every day, I gain more knowledge and insight into what works and what doesn't, which means I'm getting stronger and wiser."
- "What's the worst that can happen?"
- "This is happening *for* me, not *to* me."

When you feel like quitting, think about these statements and reflect on why your goal is so important to you. If need be, add even more reasons why. The more reasons you have to keep going, the less likely it is that you'll give up.

Just because you've been working on your goal for a while and can't yet see progress, doesn't mean nothing is happening. You may be closer to achieving your dream than you think. You could be moments away from succeeding!

REASON #3: WE SHARE OUR KNOWLEDGE GENEROUSLY

You may have met people who consider themselves "experts," yet keep their knowledge close to their chests. They're afraid to share what they know, for fear that someone will steal their ideas. *This is the opposite of nearly everyone I know in retail. We strive to make a genuine positive difference and can't help but share and teach what we have learned along the way.* I consider this book to be an example of that impulse.

The love for sharing our knowledge generously has been expressed to me on many occasions, especially when I have asked a team member to describe their favorite leader. They often thank this person for "teaching them everything they know."

We can all shape future leaders by building positive and inspired members who go on to highly successful retail careers. Even if those careers are accidental.

We can all shape future leaders by building positive and inspired members who go on to highly successful retail careers.

TRACY HEUREUX
Jewelry Sales Manager, fifteen years in retail

"Never give up your power, even when it gets hard. Never let someone know they got to you. Remain calm even in the most heated of moments."

GARTH W. JACKSON
Educator; Fashion Business and Creative Arts, twenty-four years in retail

"Retail is hard, there's no doubt about it. There are so many tough days, long days, and days we make a loss. When we haven't fulfilled a promise we made to a client, or when we've sent the wrong item to someone for a special birthday, that's when we need to be our best, not give up, and create magic."

KIM EVEN
Retail Leader, thirty+ years in retail

"We're called crazy by our families for working days and nights, weekends, and holidays! We take days to prepare for store visits that last hours, sometimes minutes. We are on the constant lookout for talent to develop and promote. We strive to create unforgettable customer experiences. Every. Single. Day. We remain calm and in control of the chaos on Black Friday, thousands of customers, hundreds of staff, gallons of coffee, and sore, tired, feet. No day is ever the same, the hustle never ends, and I wouldn't have it any other way!"

We love to teach because knowledge and education are the basis of everything we can accomplish in life and at work. All the teachers around us, personally and professionally, have played an essential role in our lives. As we teach others, we, too, inspire, support, and mentor, taking the chance to discover and share some of the best parts of ourselves.

Here are just a handful of the reasons we love to teach:

- We positively influence how others think about retail.
- Training is fun! Exposure to different skills from your peers can help you want more from yourself, engaging everybody in a game of acquiring knowledge.
- We can inspire others to build self-esteem and learn new skills, no matter their background or abilities. A well-trained team is a confident team that will likely deliver the best possible experiences to customers.
- When our team members come from various backgrounds and cultures, we can explore a diverse world. This keeps us grounded and helps us develop empathy for all.
- As we continually develop our own skills to teach others, we become lifelong learners. Sharing knowledge pushes us to get better at what we do.

- We can encourage everyone to dream, leading to big ideas, business solutions, and innovations. A great teacher can inspire a student to think beyond their comfort zone and reach their full potential.
- As I said about my grandfather in the dedication of this book, "your most significant impact may be ahead of you, and you might not even know it." For me, this is the core of why we share our knowledge generously.

Investment in training creates a workplace where teams gain access to ideas they wouldn't otherwise have discovered. Through these training opportunities, they will feel appreciated and challenged, develop high job satisfaction, and become more successful.

LEANDRA REID
Twenty years in retail

"Great training will teach those closest to your customers how to build strong connections. Discover what motivates them and dedicate your leadership to making your team the best it can be. By treating them with care every day and committing to their development, you will have high employee retention."

> **JIN HUR**
> Sales Manager, twenty-one years in retail
>
> "In a world where people communicate through screens all day, I love the real human interactions you can have when you are training. I love the power to make someone laugh or smile, and I get paid to do it."

Any successful team, big or small, has one thing at its core: effective collaboration rooted in excellent training. Celebrate your love of teaching and make an impact on someone today!

REASON #4: BECAUSE VISUAL MERCHANDISING MATTERS MORE THAN EVER

Great visual merchandising has an immediate positive impact on store shoppers. There is a direct correlation between the customer's experience and the level of detail you put into store presentation. Strong product presentation skills showcase your store in an enticing way that attracts customers and enhances your brand. Yet the objective isn't just to look good; it's to fuel sales!

I have a particular love of this aspect of our business. Maybe it's the fact that I studied both business and fashion design, the art and the commerce. As an artist and businessman, I have naturally gravitated toward

> **Visual merchandising allows you to dream, play, have fun, and be your most creative self.**

merchandising and spent several of my years at GAP in visual roles visiting stores across the country and teaching merchandising. Some of my favorite store visits were those that involved bringing the store on a journey from mediocre to *"wow this looks great!"*

Visual merchandising allows you to dream, play, have fun, and be your most creative self. Use your uniqueness and personality! It doesn't matter what role you play in the store, what company you work for, or what you sell; visual merchandising is part of your unique tool kit.

KEMOY DUHANEY
Customer Experience Strategy Consultant, seventeen years in retail

"I love that retail provides the opportunity for customers to have an experience that engages all of the five senses, that's immersive. I love that retail sparks new ideas, new connections, and new experiences."

BRANDON LEE
Director of Visual Merchandising,
fourteen years in retail

"The best leadership advice I have received
was, 'Harness that wild imagination of yours
into display.' As a creative person, this struck
home for me because it celebrated who I am
and encouraged me to embrace it and use it to
further my career. It resonated into something
important and told me that I can make a living
with creativity."

REASON #5: WE ARE ALL PART OF A VAST RETAIL FAMILY

Our retail industry offers so many unique career paths
and opportunities to work for some of the world's most
recognizable brands. Many of the goals of a retail organization—sales generation, cash flow, product innovation, and building customer relationships—intersect
with other fields like marketing, finance, technology,
loss prevention, merchandising, and management.
The possibilities are endless!

Why is this important? Because every person in
a store or company plays a unique role in its struc-
ture and function. Each individual's strengths and

personality traits contribute to the team's success, often the same way family members rely on each other for support. This dynamic can lead to a unique family culture that is a by-product of its people, processes, and resources.

This connected culture ensures your team members feel supported when they contribute ideas to grow the business, and that your teams are committed to your goals and values. The team builds community, as members take pride in their work and respect one another. With this supportive family culture, you will reach greater heights in growth, sales revenue, and profit because your team will be performing at its peak.

You are among a prosperous, powerful, hardworking group of people who lead multi-million dollar businesses.

When you think of the many teams in your life, be proud of your "retail family." You are among a prosperous, powerful, hard-working group of people who lead multi-million dollar businesses. We have a significant impact on the economy, and we're part of an unparalleled network of talent. Spend a few minutes today telling someone how proud you are and inspire a future leader to choose the same profession as you did. Invite someone into our family.

GARTH W. JACKSON
Educator; Fashion Business and Creative Arts,
twenty-four years in retail

"Retail can be a fun, fast-paced environment. You interact with so many people at different stages in their lives with drastically different needs. My friends from the retail world became my family; there is a strong mentality needed for a long retail career, and it makes you a more empathetic person."

CHRISTINE WERTMAN
Zipline Basecamp Attendant,
fifteen years in retail

"I love the way coworkers become family. Even if you don't like each other, you are still somehow bonded by the shared retail experience."

REASON #6: EVERY DAY IS DIFFERENT

I often hear that one of the greatest things about working in retail is that we never know where the day is going to take us, who will (or won't) walk through the door, what successes or challenges we might face, and how we will tackle these challenges head-on to achieve our goals.

We say "bring it on" because one of the many traits we have in common is that we are competitive in nature and love to win. The pleasure of *not* knowing what we might need to do to win that day makes things even more exciting.

Over the course of many years in retail, I have learned that the better you can adapt to an ever-changing environment, the more productive and successful you'll become. You'll handle change with ease and free up time you might otherwise have spent stressing over emerging challenges. Being flexible displays your natural leadership, determination, and analytical skills.

There are several benefits to being flexible and adaptable in the workplace, so embrace the fact that every day is different:

- You'll be a more valuable employee; when others see you embracing change, it will inspire them to do the same, and that helps the entire team.
- You'll be better equipped to face the daily challenges that invariably show up. You'll be able to effectively handle adverse situations, such as a demanding customer, without letting them get the best of you.

> **We say "bring it on" because one of the many traits we have in common is that we are competitive in nature and love to win.**

- You'll be happier and less frustrated. When you embrace change, you can find a reason to be satisfied in any situation.
- It will be easier for you to flex to career changes or new companies; every time you make a move to a new company, you will need to change how you work to meet the brand's expectations. The faster you can do this, the more successful you will be.

DOUG RICCIO
CEO, thirty-five years in retail

"I love the ever-changing direction of the retail business, and I love the uniqueness of all the people that you meet in a day."

RICK PLANOS
Consultant, twenty years in retail

"I loved my career in retail because it always provided me with something new and different every day. As my career advanced, retail took me all over the country and all over the world. I used to joke with my friends, saying, 'If they have a shopping mall, then I've been there!' My retail work has taken me to Japan, South Korea, Hong Kong, Taiwan, Indonesia, Australia, United Kingdom, Spain, Canada, Saudi Arabia, Dubai, and every single state. When I last counted, I had relocated to eleven different homes due to promotions and job changes."

- You'll be more relevant; employers want to hire people who can adapt to ongoing change with ease.

All of this is to say that we love the fact that every day is different, and that adaptability is essential to staying relevant in retail. The more adaptable you are, the more comfortable you will be embracing new ways of doing things and changing with the landscape.

REASON #7: WE ARE MOSTLY SELF-TAUGHT

One day you are a human resources manager; the next day you are styling the mannequins in the window, the day after that you are opening dozens of boxes. You think strategically and get your hands dirty at the same time. No specific college degree guarantees that you will excel at all of these things, or have the broad skillset necessary to succeed in retail.

I studied Retail Management at FIDM, but that qualification is certainly not what has kept me learning and growing over the last thirty years. *There are a variety of relevant degrees in merchandising, business, marketing, or even psychology, but most true retail field leaders are self-taught and proud of it.*

In many other industries, success is linked to education. Does being self-taught make your success less valid? Absolutely not! This can be why so many people feel that a career in retail is temporary while they wait to begin their "real profession," the one they may have studied for in college. This widespread perception is far from the truth, because a great retail leader must possess an expansive skillset, including many of the following:

- Visual merchandising expertise
- Human resources and employee relations skills
- Expert store operational knowledge
- A love of the product they sell
- The ability to motivate a team
- A passion for the customer and serving others
- Exceptional training abilities
- Loss prevention and detection
- Being a great listener

What does it mean to be self-taught? And why should you be proud of it? We no longer live in a time when information is difficult to find. Yet, the industry is still short on formal education programs for retail leaders, which puts us somewhere between self-guided and instructed. This is an excellent place to be; it's the best of both worlds.

Remember, too, that a degree doesn't represent an end to learning. Even a formal education is only meant to prepare you for a life of self-guided learning. With the power of the internet, and the mass media at your disposal, there's no reason not to follow your mind wherever it may lead.

> **It's good to be self-taught because it means you think creatively, and you're motivated to learn.**

In the end, it's not critical whether you're self-taught or formally educated. Curiosity matters more than qualifications (that's one of the pillars of success you'll

---

ORLANDO ROBLE
Store Director, ten years in retail

"I got into it for the same reason anyone gets into it. I needed a job. I was twenty-two years old and had worked full time driving heavy machinery for the past five years. But I needed a change. I got my first full-time retail job at a store I shopped at regularly. A salesperson had once joked that I should work there for the discount, so I did. I thought I'd do it for a few months, and that was ten years ago. I'm now a store director for a luxury brand, and I'm having a blast and completely self-taught."

read about in chapter 6). *It's good to be self-taught because it means you think creatively, and you're motivated to learn.*

I hold people who are self-taught in very high regard, because I believe that genius is a characteristic not of people who have an extraordinary ability to learn, but of those who are *tenacious* in their *desire* to learn.

REASON #8: THE LOVE OF THE "MILLION DOLLAR HUSTLE"

I started a business when I was about twelve years old, selling baby food jars wrapped in faux fur, with plastic bobbly eyes and a tiny hat hot-glued on top. I spent hours every day after school producing inventory, and, on the weekends, I sold hundreds of them on the front lawn. I knew that I was going to be in sales because I was good at the hustle.

Since then, I've played a role in the growth of many businesses where I joined the company in its early stages, built the foundation to scale it, and opened dozens of stores over the years. I've noticed in my career that I enjoy the energy and entrepreneurial spirit that comes with this high growth, and I thrive on being around people who love to work hard and show their hustle.

When I say "hustle," I'm not talking about shady business or selling illegal products. I'm talking about someone whose ambitions and drive are aligned. *Hustlers don't make excuses when they don't achieve their goals; they look the issue square in the eye and accept it as an opportunity to improve.*

I think you love the hustle too. I think you love the idea of maybe getting to work in one of the company flagships, making a name for yourself, and running a large business. It's incredibly challenging to build a multimillion dollar store or personal sales business in retail. In the best of times, it's a constant struggle. In the worst of times, it can feel like a losing battle. Is that a reason to give up? Hell no.

> **Hustlers don't make excuses when they don't achieve their goals; they look the issue square in the eye and accept it as an opportunity to improve.**

If you're at all serious about building a multimillion dollar business, you need to be self-motivated and not wait for someone to tell you what to do. Period. Throughout my career, I have worked with and led dozens of "million-dollar sellers." They're some of the hardest working, most dedicated people in stores. Their energy, drive, and hustle are unparalleled, yet so is their humility. They're the ones whose accidental careers we should celebrate. If you're one of them, you are the foundation of any great retail company and the customer experience, and I thank you.

Most business leaders agree that no one can hit the million-dollar target individually or as a store without hard work, a smart strategy, and laser-sharp focus. Whether you work in a $3 million store or a $30 million flagship, it's a complicated business that requires a wide range of skills from every person on the team. Call it what you want, I call it the million-dollar hustle. Be proud of it!

> **KIM EVEN**
> Retail Leader, thirty+ years in retail
>
> "Let me tell you about the hustle! Shipment, floor set, markdowns, windows, conference calls, sales reporting, ad sets, replenishment, client outreach, product training, phones ringing, emails pinging, morning huddles, and a coffee run, all before 10 a.m."

REASON #9: WE CREATE FRIENDSHIPS THAT CAN LAST DECADES

This reason is very special to me. The majority of my closest friendships are with people I have worked with in some capacity over many years. In many cases, there was an instant connection. I am forever grateful to call these people my friends.

There is something special about all of the reasons listed in this chapter, but lifelong friendships are the most beautiful part

> **Good relationships with others in our vast retail family are also necessary as we grow our careers. These connections will always serve us well in the future.**

of my career. And there is most definitely love there. *Good relationships with others in our vast retail family are also necessary as we grow our careers. These connections will always serve us well in the future.*

A network of people who know and respect you can also provide you with credibility and a reputation for excellence. You might join a company and then think about bringing someone along from your past. There are always opportunities both ways. Often, something that begins as a mentorship can turn into a peer relationship for years to come.

Whether it's for your dream job or just the next best thing for you, don't forget the connections you've made thus far. They are every bit as important as your next adventure. Keep things positive, and you can be sure that everyone will remember you as a significant part of the team.

KIM EVEN
Retail Leader, thirty+ years in retail

"Some of my best friends are people I've met at work. I'm still friends with most of them ten, twenty, and (gulp) almost thirty years later, including you, Ron. Working in a relationship-building industry, it makes sense that we have close relationships with our coworkers. My work friends have supported me through challenges and cheered me to success. We've traveled the world, celebrated promotions, graduations, marriage, birth, and mourned death, and divorce. Only a coworker understands the context, the passion, and sometimes the rants. These relationships strengthen us because we can do what we do best with people we appreciate. In our unpredictable world, challenging times are unavoidable. These friendships enable us to face these challenges and persevere."

REASON #10: BECAUSE FOR MANY OF US, RETAIL IS AN ACCIDENTAL CAREER

Have you ever heard someone talk about "just falling into their career?" That somehow, they got to where they are today by accident? How many people do you know who embarked on their dream job as soon as they

TOD HALLMAN
Fashion Stylist

"In the early 1980s, The Beverly Center was a new concept mall and the premier shopping center in Los Angeles, where I met you, Ron. I didn't know it then, but it would become one of the most important groups of friends in my young life. Now, over thirty years later, even though we're not all together, we are the best of friends, and when we see one another, it's like we are in our twenties all over again. These are the friends that I met by chance, working in retail. But what I found were relationships that have lasted me far past my early retail adventure and have become lifetime friends that I cherish and hold so profoundly in my heart."

finished their education? Probably not very many. In reality, most people take time to decide on their calling, if indeed they find one. Some people float from one job to the next before suddenly realizing years have passed, and they're halfway up a ladder in a career they feel ambivalent about.

Which brings me to the accidental career in retail. Rarely do people say, "If things are going well when I graduate, I'd like to land a job at the mall." That's not how it starts. There's often a part-time job in college while they're studying something completely unrelated, and then they get bitten by the retail bug. If they're lucky enough to have a great leader, or in my case, several, it can lead to the decision to make retail a career.

Grit, hard work, hustle, pride, empathy, curiosity, and focus. Whatever you choose to call it, the magic ingredient for retail career success and satisfaction is self-determination.

Grit, hard work, hustle, pride, empathy, curiosity, and focus. Whatever you choose to call it, the magic ingredient for retail career success and satisfaction is self-determination. When you fully commit to retail, it stops being an accidental career. You become the captain of your beautiful ship and get to decide which way to sail.

WAS THIS AN ACCIDENTAL CAREER?

ELIZABETH "EK" KORCZYKOWSKI
Boutique Director, eighteen years in retail

"Yes! I wanted to be an actress. My first retail leadership opportunity presented itself to me, and I realized that the curtain goes up every day. I still get to command the attention of the room and try to make people smile!"

WAS THIS AN ACCIDENTAL CAREER?

LISA MOLINARI
Corporate Sales Manager, twenty years in retail

"Yes! I was recruited off of the sales floor where I loved to shop. I remember thinking, 'this will be cool, and I'll get a good discount.' Never be afraid of the hustle or hard work; leadership came to me quickly. I was a trusted and loyal employee who embraced the customer experience and was a natural-born seller."

KEMOY DUHANEY
Customer Experience Strategy Consultant, seventeen years in retail

"As a first-generation college student of Jamaican-American heritage, retail wasn't one of the accepted prosperous career paths. It was viewed as a job to provide supplemental income while I was in school, 'studying for my real career.' Most of the adults around me were hard working, but I didn't recall anyone who loved their career. My journey as a retail leader has been one of the most rewarding and fulfilling experiences of my life, and I saw how much value my leadership provided to my team and customers. I felt it was my duty to 'legitimize' this career path for others. There are so many talented, purposeful, disciplined leaders ready to be discovered and developed."

You decide how to spend every year, every month, and every day of your precious time. You get to choose when to let other people steer your ship and when to grab the wheel. Now is the time to take control of your career, even if it's accidental!

PART II

THE THREE PILLARS

OF RETAIL EXPERTISE: EMPATHY, CURIOSITY, AND FOCUS

EMPATHY AND HUMAN CONNECTION START WHEN YOU PUT THE HONEST CONVERSATION YOU NEED TO HAVE AT THE TOP OF YOUR PRIORITY LIST.

CHAPTER 3

THE FIRST PILLAR

EMPATHY IS AT THE CORE OF SERVING OTHERS

Humans are, at our core, social beings, and we thrive in interactions with others.

As far back as we can trace, humans traveled, hunted, and built shelters in social groups, and for good reason. Social activities allow us to engage with one another and develop essential communication skills. In this part of the book, *I want to demonstrate that communication in all its forms is at the core of retail.*

Empathy is defined as *"the capacity to comprehend and share another person's feelings."* It is about standing in someone else's shoes, listening with our heart, and understanding their needs. It allows us to create meaningful connections with others. And it helps us sell products and services that people love. It helps us listen, connect, and grow.

Communication rooted in empathy helps us connect on a deeper level and is crucial to human interaction, be it a personal relationship that has lasted for years or a conversation with a customer you have just met on the sales floor.

The more quickly you can connect with those around you, the more likely they are to trust in your ability to answer their questions and offer solutions and recommendations. Empathy enables you to step out of your world and into someone else's.

I encourage you to play your part in creating an environment where empathy, maybe even more than sales productivity, is rewarded. You'll find that encouraging the former just might improve the latter.

But where do you start? First, let's explore how to demonstrate empathy with each other, and then I will share thoughts on how empathy is critical to serving your customers.

HAVE HONEST CONVERSATIONS

The bonds we create with each other are vital to building our businesses. As I discussed earlier, these connections can be one of the primary reasons we love working in retail, and they can last decades. However, in a retail environment full of distractions, it can be hard to build strong relationships when we have limited time.

> Communication rooted in empathy helps us connect on a deeper level and is crucial to human interaction, be it a personal relationship that has lasted for years or a conversation with a customer you have just met on the sales floor.

Having honest conversations is even more challenging now that so much of our communication happens via emails and text messages. We all benefit from social media because it provides a way to connect and create a community in the absence of in-person contact. But while these digital tools help us stay in touch with each other, essential and emotional conversations are sometimes hard to navigate in a virtual context.

There are times when we want to say what's in our hearts, and it can be challenging to know where to start. It might be scary to open up about things that really matter to us, personally or professionally. *Empathy and human connection start when you put the honest conversation you need to have at the top of your priority list.*

HOW TO PUT IT TO WORK

Talk with, not about: The easiest ways to *avoid* discussing a difficult topic is to focus on people who are not present. When discussing someone who's not in the room, you're looking past the person who's right in front of you. Don't miss the opportunity to direct your attention to the experiences and feelings of those who are present.

Speak from your heart: We can talk about our favorite subjects all day: fashion, technology, sports, pets, and kids. We can also conceal ourselves behind these topics, never delving more in-depth into why and how they touch our lives in meaningful ways.

Determining when it's safe to introduce your real feelings into a conversation takes sensitivity, bravery, and a willingness to experiment. If your conversation partner expresses interest in your personal feelings and experiences, you'll likely feel confident sharing more. On the other hand, you'll know quickly if they are not able or willing to go deeper. Remember that it's always important to find people with whom you can share how you really feel and speak honestly.

Listen from your heart: Just as you must be courageous enough to tell your own stories and express your own concerns, you must also be open enough to listen to someone else's.

Deep listening isn't easy. It requires concentration, compassion, and self-awareness. You know how good it feels when you realize someone clearly hears what you have to say, and how bad it feels when the other person seems distracted, more interested in sharing their own perspective, or intent on "fixing" you.

When your conversation partner says something that triggers a strong emotion, whether that be sadness, envy, boredom, or excitement, challenge yourself to stay present rather than insert yourself into the narrative. When that person struggles with a challenge that seems to have an obvious solution, resist the impulse to give advice. Keep listening. Recognize your own motivations and try to focus on the other person.

Keep practicing: Even if the only thing you want from a conversation with someone else is a deeper connection, you may not get it. Insisting on such an outcome when a person is not interested or emotionally ready isn't just ineffective, it's unkind.

It takes courage to initiate authentic and empathetic conversations, to say to someone, *"This is how I feel; this is what I need. Would you be willing to go there with me?"* Similarly, it takes bravery to let go of what you've hoped for in a conversation and not be frustrated.

It also takes practice. *The more you seek to empathize with others, the more you will hone your skills.* You will learn to approach your honest conversations with greater patience and compassion. Over time, your relationships will feel less like a series of casual chats and more like the authentic connections you need.

DEVELOP THE SKILLS YOU NEED TO CONNECT WITH ANYONE YOU MEET

In the retail environment, each day brings us opportunities to meet new people. Connecting with empathy helps us be better coworkers, better leaders, and better friends. The ability to connect with a person you just met moments ago is an opportunity to create common ground. It points the conversation in a direction that was not possible without it.

Connecting with people who are similar to us is relatively easy. When we have common interests and personalities, we "get" each other; it can even be effortless. Building relationships with people who are very different from us, however, can be quite challenging. Yet, as we learn and grow, it's essential to engage with people who have different strengths than we do.

HOW TO PUT IT TO WORK

What's your name? Not everyone is gifted at putting names to faces. It can be particularly challenging to remember names if you are in a social setting or store environment where you're meeting a lot of people in a short amount of time. But remembering people's names and being able to address them directly will instantly make them feel acknowledged and welcomed.

Learn how to tell your own connection story: Make yourself memorable by having a story to tell about yourself that gives insight into who you are and what you're about. If you're an aspiring artist, designer, singer, or writer, come up with a narrative about why this is important to you and what experiences have fueled your desires and life goals.

Your *connection story* should be specific and refer to important events and people in your life. It should also make others feel comfortable sharing their stories with you. Use this to give people a glimpse into who you are and what you believe. Telling stories captures people's attention better than rattling off facts and numbers about the results of your store.

Add value to the conversation: Find ways to make yourself invaluable, and people will appreciate you. Being of service to others, even in small ways, is a great way to connect.

Maybe you have a tip on a job opening or a referral to someone looking for services your conversational partner can offer. It could be something as small as lending them a book or telling them about a great TED talk on a topic they are interested in.

Share what's important to you: We all have thoughts, ideas, beliefs, and goals. Be willing to share a bit of yourself—who you are and what you believe in—and others will naturally be curious and want to engage with you. Have you done something unique? Are you passionate about a cause? People will find you more interesting and memorable if they know what makes you tick.

DEMONSTRATING EMPATHY WITH YOUR CUSTOMERS WILL GROW YOUR BUSINESS

It's not enough to just sell a product. People want to make a connection with you, your team, and your brand.

But we all know how difficult it can be to do this in a highly demanding store environment. No doubt you've heard the mantra time and time again: *exceptional customer service is the key to your store/company's long-term success and growth.* It sounds simple, but it's so much more complicated than you'd think!

> Exceptional customer service is the key to your store/company's long-term success and growth.

Most companies still assume that customer service is simply about asking questions like "are you finding everything okay?" or "is there anything specific you are looking for?" I am here to say that's not good enough.

Understanding why your customer walked in the door is one step in creating a store experience. But the process *really* begins well before they arrive, and companies that "get it" take the time to understand their customers in a deep and meaningful way. They make a concerted effort to apply consumer insight to every aspect of their business, from new product development and call center training to store environments. These companies are consistent in their approach across all touchpoints, and their customers appreciate the effort.

It's not enough to just sell a product. People want to make a connection with you, your team, and your brand.

Throughout this journey, your role at the store is arguably your most important one. Working in a customer-facing role gives you a great opportunity to build meaningful connections. The power is in your hands to craft a message that encapsulates every aspect of the brand and solidifies the notion that the customer is at the center of the experience.

Every business transaction, every sale, needs to involve a genuine and authentic connection between a brand and its customers. It's not always a deep relationship, but it's a relationship, nevertheless.

HOW TO PUT IT TO WORK

Get back to your Zen: Crossed arms, heavy sighs, short replies—you know when a customer's getting frustrated. Worse, these physical signs show they're losing interest in what you're saying, and your shot at keeping their business might be fading fast.

So, put your excellent communication skills to work, draw on your superpower of reading the situation, and use empathy to diffuse the situation. Here are some key phrases I use to do that:

- "I can understand how frustrating it is when..."
- "I realize how complicated it is to..."
- "I imagine how upsetting it is to..."
- "I know how confusing it must be when..."
- "I'm so sorry to hear that..."

Become the customer: One of my favorite best practices is to send my team out to explore competitors and other service businesses as a customer. That experiment almost always changes perceptions of what empathy and service can look like. Walking a mile in a customer's shoes is the fastest way to gain insight into their perspective and understand how they experience you and your store.

Just smile: It may sound simple but smiling when talking to customers can make a substantial positive impact. It comes across over the phone, too. When you smile, customers can hear it in your voice. Smiling improves your mood and the mood of everyone around you. We tend to mimic the emotions of those around us, so when you smile, you naturally improve the customer experience.

Put empathy before sales: Selling and retail are arts, and the most successful salespeople don't try to pitch a product or service relentlessly. Top salespeople recognize that their customers have limited time and multiple options. They strive to create a consistent, positive experience by being courteous and professional throughout the customer journey. This can result in higher sales results and repeat business over time.

Show that you care: *Being genuine and kind will never go out of style, and costs you absolutely nothing.* If you are uplifting and positive, and show common courtesy to those around you, you will begin building bonds beyond business.

Caring about the people who buy what you sell is the key to success in sales. Period. Dale Carnegie, the American writer and developer of courses in self-improvement, public speaking, and interpersonal skills, said it best: "You can make more friends in two months by becoming interested in other people than you can in two years by trying to get other people interested in you."

LET'S WRAP IT UP

"People don't care how much you know until they know how much you care." This quote has been attributed to many people over the years, including President Theodore Roosevelt, John Maxwell, and Earl Nightingale. It's a statement we can all relate to, especially in a conversation about empathy.

The next time you find yourself in a meeting, on a call, or in conversation with a customer or coworker, try committing to listening, asking questions, and being curious enough to show that you really do care about them personally. By doing this, you will demonstrate a greater level of empathy. It's a pillar of retail success!

YOUR ABILITY TO CREATE VALUE FOR YOUR TEAM AND YOUR CUSTOMERS STARTS WITH BEING CURIOUS.

CHAPTER 4

THE SECOND PILLAR

THE ROAD TO A GREAT RETAIL CAREER IS PAVED WITH CURIOSITY

If empathy is the first pillar of retail expertise, curiosity is the second. Albert Einstein famously said, *"I have no special talents. I am only passionately curious."* Whatever your current role or your dream role, the road to being great at retail sales or leadership is paved with curiosity.

Your ability to create value for your team and your customers starts with being curious. You have to seek to understand how things work, why people do things a certain way, why people want what they want, and when it makes sense to take action.

Curious people are often more open to new ideas, enabling them to approach challenges and people more empathetically. In fact, I believe the best thing a company can do to promote inclusion is to hire very curious leaders. They will likely be more willing to understand and connect with people who are different, creating more diverse teams and inclusive cultures.

The best retail people I have known, in both sales and leadership, have devoted their lives to finding new solutions to old problems, new ways to motivate people, new ways to think, and even new ways to interact.

The best retail people I have known, in both sales and leadership, have devoted their lives to finding new solutions to old problems, new ways to motivate people, new ways to think, and even new ways to interact.

While some people believe that once they have found a solution, they can stop looking for new ideas, great retailers tirelessly go on pursuing the latest and the best. These are the people I like to surround myself with. Their qualities are ones I aspire to embody myself.

When I was young and first started selling, I developed the practice of asking my customers a lot of questions. At first, the questions were direct: "what do you do?" or "tell me about your closet."

Both of these were important because I was selling luxury men's suiting, and my knowledge base was far inferior to that of my customers. Still, I was curious to learn how to make them happy, and that covered up for any lack of skill I may have had at the time.

At some point, I recognized that creating a service that was of higher value for my customers meant learning more about each of their professional businesses. I started asking different, more specific questions to obtain a real understanding of their line of work and the role that their wardrobe played in their success. Over time I understood what each of my customers needed, when they needed it, and what they liked. All because I was curious.

A curious mind is invaluable in such a complex environment. It allows you to imagine creative new solutions and ways to deal with your team and customers.

Retail environments provide endless opportunities to learn. It all starts with you and what you are passionate about. You might find interest in understanding the merchandise on the floor better, getting to know the store operations more deeply, or digging into the back-of-the-house processes. You might find that researching competitors or learning more about the products your company sells helps you get a better understanding of your business.

A curious mind is invaluable in such a complex environment. Not only does it deepen your knowledge of what exists, but more importantly, it allows you to imagine creative new solutions and ways to deal with your team and customers.

HOW TO PUT IT TO WORK

Don't be afraid of the unknown: *In exploratory sales conversations, the depth and breadth of what you discover depends on the quality of questions you ask.* Maybe you can help the client learn something new about themselves at the same time. Taking care of your customer requires the curiosity to understand why things are done a certain way before taking action.

I remember the relief I felt when I joined Apple as a new store manager. Part of their incredible culture is the idea that no one person is an expert at everything. Apple encourages the use of "I don't know, let's find out" to engage with the customer, a response rooted in both curiosity and empathy. I still use this today whenever I get stuck because it creates a sense of collaboration and discovery.

The best salespeople have an insatiable desire to learn, and they don't allow temporary setbacks to distract them from their highest aspirations. Curiosity gives us the power to push through uncertainty, ask tough questions, and build our decision-making skills.

Results can't drive every decision: When a company sees its customers merely as dollar signs, they often treat them as a metric. And customers know it. Most large companies record key performance indicators such as conversion rates or a variety of other results that track each customer's dollar value and relationship to sales. While these can be useful to understand, don't let them drive your decision-making.

Great companies appreciate their customers as the most valuable assets (aside from the team), treat them like human beings, worry about them, and strive to give them a fantastic experience. They are always interested in knowing what customers think, and they use that feedback to drive decision-making.

Surround yourself with curious people: *If you want to be better at sales, a more effective leader,*

or an all-around more successful person, surround
yourself with interesting people who welcome
surprise into their lives. They like to try a new
food, talk to a stranger, or ask a question they've
never asked before. The best team to work on is
one full of curious people!

Take the time to pay attention to and be
interested to learn more about your coworkers.
You're with these people every day. During
downtime, why not take a moment to develop
a deeper understanding of who they are? It's a
great way to improve your team relationships.

Keep asking for feedback: Customer feedback
is vital because it can serve as a guiding resource
for the growth of your store or company. Don't
you want to know what you're getting right,
and maybe wrong, in the eyes of the customer?
You can find gems in that feedback that will
make it easier to adjust and adapt the customer
experience over time. Feedback is the way to
keep your team and your customer at the heart of
everything you do.

Never be blinded by your own passion for
your product: You may think a specific product
needs to be used one way, but your customers
may have something else to say entirely. Take the

opportunity to solicit a different opinion, even if you don't like it. Product blindness is just one symptom of not asking enough questions. I find this particularly true in the fashion space, where many sales associates love the newest trends so much that they are blind to the realities of an individual customer's tastes.

Don't be distracted by the competition: Obsessing about what everyone else is doing will inevitably lead to anxiety. This may cause you to mentally put a dollar sign above the head of every customer, creating a lack of success and all of the stress that comes with it. Companies with a clear purpose set the tone in their respective industries because they lead with curiosity. Others look to follow *them*, not the other way around.

Educate yourself about ideas outside of traditional retail: Steve Jobs studied beautiful objects and wanted all his products to be highly attractive. Could his products have been as successful if they simply worked well? Possibly, but his curiosity made Apple products unique in the marketplace.

The innovations or ideas that you're searching for might already exist in other sectors. Ask yourself, "what other industries face a similar problem?" *I most often derive inspiration not from other retailers, but from the luxury restaurant or hotel businesses whose entire reputation hinges on their customer experience.*

Study disruption before it's too late: The hotel industry encountered it with Airbnb. The taxi and black car industry faced it with Uber. The music industry faced it with Spotify. Everywhere you look, industries are being disrupted. *Retail is no exception.* Studying what is happening in the industry will always serve you well.

Each of those companies provided a service that was more convenient than the tried-and-true methods. By doing so, they changed the game for their users and competitors. In the case of brick-and-mortar retail, the shark in the water is e-commerce, especially behemoths like Amazon.

The best physical stores center obsessively on their core value proposition and innovate new ways to drive store traffic and build customer loyalty. These initiatives may be expensive, but the brands that invest for the long term will have a better chance of retaining relevance.

Never settle: While other people might keep applying ideas that have worked well enough in the past, be on the lookout for dramatic shifts in the industry. Never settle for what *"always worked in the past."* When you arrive at the mountaintop, do not settle! Find a higher mountain. When you break a new record, do not settle. Go beyond it! When you finally win that fight, that job, or that sale, do not settle!

LET'S WRAP IT UP

I often get asked what the secret ingredient to success is, and while everyone has their own answer—like hard work, dedication, or persever- ance—there is one that I believe leads to more success than oth- ers. That ingredient is curios- ity. The most successful people I know, whose successes are not just financial, are naturally curious, which leads them to new ventures, new solutions, new achievements, and new beginnings.

> **Great companies appreciate their customers as the most valuable assets (aside from the team), treat them like human beings, worry about them, and strive to give them a fantastic experience.**

Think about how much you might miss if you already assume you know where your journey will take you! *Curiosity leads to learning and learning fuels curiosity.* Not everything you discover will be of interest, but don't let that put you off developing that skill. In the next decade of exceptional retail, curiosity will light the way.

WHAT CAN WE DO TO FOCUS ON THE THINGS THAT MATTER AND IGNORE THE THINGS THAT DON'T?

CHAPTER 5

THE THIRD PILLAR

WHAT YOU FOCUS ON BECOMES YOUR GREATEST POWER

Leading stores and teams for more than two decades, I have come to the realization that focus is simply the ability to distinguish the "nice things to do" from the "must do." It's much more than just a word on a job description. It's a way of life and constant practice, and when done well, it can become your most significant power.

When our focus is consistent, it allows us to begin something without procrastination and then maintain our effort until the mission is complete. It helps us pay attention amid distractions and setbacks, sustaining the energy needed to reach a goal.

Focus is important because it's the path to so many other brain functions: perception, memory, learning, reasoning, problem-solving, and decision-making. Without it, our thoughts are scattered. While it's fun to daydream on occasion, if we can't think effectively, we definitely can't produce the quality of work necessary for success.

Focus is important because it's the path to so many other brain functions: perception, memory, learning, reasoning, problem-solving, and decision-making.

In the retail environment, focusing on specific tasks can be especially challenging and can look different every day. If you have felt overwhelmed, you are not alone. The list of things to get done is rarely short, the payroll hours might be lower than they were last year, you had someone call out today for an important shift—the list of challenges goes on.

That is why I believe that the last of the three pillars of retail expertise is focus. There is no question that what we focus on will impact significant positive change in our business. Now for the big question: *what can we do to focus on the things that matter and ignore the things that don't?* In an environment of constant distraction, how can we hone our focus?

To answer that question, let's consider some of the observable strengths of someone who is highly focused in the retail environment:

- Exceptional communication skills—positive influence starts with excellent communication.
- The ability to think critically—skillfully conceptualizing, applying, analyzing, and evaluating information.
- Influence upward with senior leadership, laterally with peers, and down to every level.
- Foresight: not playing just for today's results, but for the week, month, quarter, and year.
- Determination: focused people keep their eyes on the prize and don't give up when it gets hard.
- Excellent time management skills: focused people watch the finish line as they watch the hour.
- Organization and planning, while remaining spontaneous enough to handle unexpected challenges.

If someone were to demonstrate at least half of these behaviors, I think their leader would say that person is focused. They may even say that the person is ready for more responsibility.

One of the lessons I have personally learned is that working on too many things at once and spreading my influence across too many platforms does not enable me to achieve the best results. I now understand how critical it is to focus on my strengths, delegate as needed, and find the power to work on fewer tasks but do them all really well. This is how I do my most productive work and get my best results!

You are always surrounded by situations and people that could stall your momentum, including technology that threatens to monopolize your attention.

You are always surrounded by situations and people that could stall your momentum, including technology that threatens to monopolize your attention. If you struggle with focus, here are some ideas to help you master this third pillar of expertise.

HOW TO PUT IT TO WORK

Have a plan for the day: Make a list of your top priorities for the day, week, month, and even year. It will help you resist reacting to every distraction that comes up. Review your list each morning and decide, realistically, what tasks you can accomplish that day. Make your plan clear. For example: *"I'm going to finish the first three items on this checklist by noon."*

From there, decide how long each item on your list takes. Some may take fifteen minutes or less. Group those things together and check them off quickly. Longer projects and more in-depth conversations will require greater focus. Make a reasonable estimate of how long each will take and try to hold yourself accountable. If you get off track, that's okay. Readjust and keep moving forward. Don't lose your focus on the big picture.

Create a space that keeps you focused: Wherever possible, find a way to carve out time when you will not be available to others, in a space where you know you can focus. This will help you go deeper into your work without having to maintain the many moving parts of your business.

When you can find these opportunities, create a specific goal for the time. For example, *"For the next sixty minutes, I am going to attentively listen to a recommended podcast on leadership."* A clear purpose will allow you to achieve your goals and gain the satisfaction that comes from being focused and present.

Schedule time to be unproductive: The pings, vibrations, and other notifications that signify the arrival of a voicemail, email, text message, or social media update can be a constant distraction. Perhaps the best thing you can do to stay on schedule is to turn off your technology and focus without interruption.

Discipline yourself to log in only when you have an extra chunk of time free. When you check social media, there is a high likelihood that you'll stay on much longer than planned because something new, exciting, and fun comes up on your feed. This is not what you need when you're focusing.

Don't say yes to everything. Highly focused people are not always people pleasers. They don't feel the need to say yes to everything. They know you can't always make everyone happy and sometimes they have to say no. Highly focused people, therefore, firmly but gently say no to things that don't help them achieve their goals, allowing them to focus on things that are important.

Stop procrastinating: We all procrastinate. The thing about procrastination is that it doesn't have an endpoint. Things keep getting postponed until tomorrow. If you leave a task that is due today until tomorrow, you will find it hard to focus on whatever you are doing. Become a pro at doing things quickly and easily, without procrastinating. To keep yourself interested, reward yourself when you accomplish the tasks at hand.

Practice developing your focus: Meditation is a great way to do this because it's just you and your thoughts. If that's not your thing, practice single-tasking throughout your day. At lunch, just eat. Don't read the newspaper or check your email at the same time. In meetings, don't doodle in your notebook or play with your phone. Focus on the meeting.

Pay attention to what is going on in your body and mind: Start to notice when and how you get distracted. What thoughts happen just before you do? Are you tired, hungry, or bored? As you learn what triggers your distraction, you can notice it and head it off at the pass before you slip into an unproductive hour-long text chat.

Just as the quality of food you eat affects your health, the ideas that fill your mind affect your mentality. If you watch television channels airing constant bad news, your perception will shift. If you do things that don't support your higher development, the quality of your awareness will decline. If your relationships are nourishing and filled with purpose, meaning, and love, that will enrich your consciousness.

Rest, relax, and recharge. Zone out with Netflix, enjoy a glass of wine, play with the dog, whatever you do to decompress. Be content knowing that you accomplished a lot today!

Making time to take care of yourself is an important part of being focused. Proper rest, good food, and time for unwinding are all necessary for a happy, healthy you. Especially when you're feeling scattered or life is chaotic like it can be in retail. Taking time for self-care gives us a chance to step back, re-group and put our needs first for a little while.

Always find fun in what you do: *Being focused and influential doesn't mean you have to be boring and serious!* When was the last time you really had fun at work? When did you last forget about all of your daily responsibilities and live in the moment? I bet you were highly focused. Think about it this way: before starting anything, ask yourself *why* you need to do it. From there, allow your creativity and imagination to get involved in the process, finding ways to make the task fun.

GOING DEEPER: PRACTICING FOCUS IN EVERY ASPECT OF THE BUSINESS

I would like to offer a more in-depth outlook on focus in our retail environment. One that might give you a fresh perspective on anything you do; I know it has for me!

When I walk into a store, the first thing I do is look at the big picture—the immediate vibe, the team dynamic, the flow of

Being focused and influential doesn't mean you have to be boring and serious!

the sales floor, visual merchandising, window displays... The list goes on and on. But what I look for more importantly, is the intention and focus behind each of these elements.

For someone who has never worked in retail, it's easy to overlook the amount of hard work that goes into building an outstanding store experience. A company that lacks focus in decision-making—from product offering and merchandising to the way back of the house is organized—finds it hard to achieve excellence.

For example, even if you have clear guidelines for merchandising your store, being focused means you can identify when something is not working and fix it. Your attention to detail is one of the most valuable factors in your store's success. When you start looking at everything with intention, and challenge the work of every task, not only will you accomplish your goals with ease, you will be able to perform the tasks even more efficiently next time. You may also think of solutions no one has thought about before.

I would also argue that focus is a unique character trait for each and every person. The way I pay attention to details is different than the way you do, and that's what makes your point of view so much more valuable to the team. Use it to your advantage! Find your focus and start changing the world!

AND LASTLY, IT GOES WITHOUT SAYING TO NEVER LOSE FOCUS ON THE CUSTOMER

The most successful salespeople I know are those who never lose focus on the customer. It's that simple. Once the initial connection is made, they shift their attention to intently listening, learning, and reiterating to the customer that they understand their needs.

It takes a tremendous amount of focus to ignore all the distractions a store can offer, whether it's a coworker who needed help a minute ago or another customer who just walked in the door. There will always be things that pull you away from the customer in front of you.

Your ability to deliver an excellent service experience depends solely on how focused you are in every interaction.

The best part is that being focused with a customer can be a by-product of approaching everyone with empathy and curiosity. When you put yourself in the customer's shoes, learn to understand their needs, and leading with a curious mind, you will discover that you have ultimately been focused and tuned.

Focus is a unique character trait for each and every person, and that's what makes your point of view so much more valuable to the team. Use it to your advantage!

LET'S WRAP IT UP

Over this chapter and the previous two, you have read about my three primary pillars of retail expertise—*empathy, curiosity, and focus*. There are dozens of other competencies that are important to anyone's success, but I can confidently say that without these three, none of the others matter. They are the foundation upon which all other skills are built.

When I am feeling my most successful, I know that I am empathetic with my team. I am curious about what's happening in the business and with the customer. And I am focused on using my valuable time productively.

When I struggle, it's because I am unclear about my direction or unwilling to learn how everyone around me feels. I might take information at face value without taking the time to learn more. At worst, I may be entirely distracted by technology, friends, or my emotions. If one of the three pillars is not standing up straight, something feels off, and I'm not at my best.

My recommendation is to use these three concepts as filters to guide your attention. When you are empathetic, curious, and focused, you know that you're on the right track to doing your best. When you have mastered them, you will be well on your way to unlocking potential that you may not know you have!

PART III

FOR
LEADERS
AND
DREAMERS

WE ALL CAN EXERCISE LEADERSHIP, EVEN IF THE WORD "LEADER" ISN'T CURRENTLY IN YOUR JOB TITLE.

CHAPTER 6

RON'S FOUNDATIONS OF GREAT RETAIL LEADERSHIP

There are hundreds, even thousands, of excellent books on leadership, and I have read many of them. Most are good, some are great, and a few have gone on to become business classics. These are the ones every aspiring leader reads. Books like *Good to Great* by Jim Collins, *The Seven Habits of Highly Effective People* by Stephen Covey, and *The One Minute Manager* by Ken Blanchard.

After reading these books, I tried to apply their ideas in my daily work in retail leadership. Sometimes I was successful, sometimes not so much.

Part of the reason the messages of these books didn't always stick with me is that the world of brick-and-mortar retail differs significantly from a typical corporate environment. Those of us in retail leadership are not sitting at a desk all day; we are catching fly balls! The skills that we need to develop are various. Some are emotional, others are tactical. They evolve over time, and a good leader will consistently cultivate new skills as their career grows.

Here's the reality: none of the books mentioned above focus specifically on retail teams. This one does. My mantra for this book is *"for retail teams and leaders, by a retail leader." My goal is to share everything I have learned about the industry from a store leadership perspective, and to offer some simple advice to anyone in retail who needs a new source of inspiration.*

Your leadership style will always be evolving, depending on what's relevant to you and your company at that particular time. Great retail companies don't restrict themselves to a single approach to success. They are multidimensional and fluid. They encourage leadership that emphasizes the importance of feedback at every level, from stores to the corporate office and back.

This part of the book is addressed explicitly to current and aspiring retail leaders. That's why it's called "For

Leaders and Dreamers." However, anyone can use these ideas to improve their performance and build their career. The following chapter describes the ideas that you can use to create a culture that allows everyone to thrive.

Whatever level you're at today, it's important to realize that we all can exercise leadership, even if the word "leader" isn't currently in your job title.

HAVE AN OPTIMISTIC ATTITUDE

The world doesn't need you to be like everyone else. You are amazing and unique, and you enjoy the fun that working in retail brings every day.

One of the most admirable attributes of great retail leaders is the abundant positivity that energizes everyone around them. It's not that they never have moments of frustration or disappointment, but they're able to take a positive approach and tackle challenging issues with ease and optimism.

Retail leaders are frequently self-taught, and our pride in developing and applying new skills creates positivity. This optimistic attitude is foundational to great leadership.

The most optimistic and inspiring leaders know how to turn setbacks into successes. They make a point to display positive traits every day. *When I reflect on the best leaders I have known, they consistently chose an optimistic approach.*

Seeing challenges as opportunities rather than obstacles is one of the most critical qualities you can display with your team. The good news is that positivity seems to be in abundance in retail environments! As we discussed in the first part of this book, *retail leaders are frequently self-taught, and our pride in developing and applying new skills creates positivity. This optimistic attitude is foundational to great leadership, so let's explore how to build some new habits.*

HOW TO PUT IT TO WORK

Create a routine: Routines get a bad rap, but they can be a powerful tool in generating optimism. I wrote this book by forming a habit of writing every morning at 6 a.m.; creating a pattern kept me optimistic that I could actually finish. Crafting a routine will help you get your most critical work done and maintain a healthy rhythm, lower stress levels and positive thinking.

Take responsibility: Have you ever noticed how people give someone an easier time when they admit they made a mistake? When somebody owns their mistake, we see a little of ourselves in them. We know that we all make mistakes, too, so we are more likely to respond with empathy and compassion. Acknowledging and accepting fallibility improves the quality of relationships, helping people relate to one another and forge bonds. This, in turn, creates positivity and optimism.

Don't sweat the small stuff: Some things will always cause frustration. Whether it's a customer having a tough day or managing coworkers struggling to get along, you can predict many of the circumstances that will rile you. In these situations, decide on your response in advance. You can't change another person. You can, however, change the direction of a conversation or change your perspective.

Use positive language: Words have energy. Use words that inspire, rather than those that spark unnecessary fireworks. Words like *hope*, *appreciate*, and *care* get situations moving much more effectively than words like *impossible, alone,* and *pessimistic.*

Bring the energy: Perhaps that means getting an extra hour of sleep at night or having an extra cup of coffee in the morning like I do. Either way, being the person who brings energy and life into the store can make you a more desirable leader. Positive energy is contagious! You don't have to be entering the store doing jumping jacks, but you don't want to show up to work completely exhausted.

SHANNON SMITH
Assistant Store Manager, thirty-five years in retail

"I am the leader I am today because of that positivity and pride. An effective leader is a person who drives someone to be better than who they were yesterday."

DANA PEREZ-ELHAI
Director of Business Development, twenty-two years in retail

"When you work in retail be willing to do whatever is needed to support everyone on the team. Find a way to bring positive energy each and every day!"

TELL PEOPLE WHAT YOU STAND FOR

No matter their role, great retail leaders start by letting everyone know what they stand for. What does that mean? On the surface, it's a simple question. However, what we stand for can often get crowded out by noise and other distractions. And I understand how many of those you have in one day in the store!

We get distracted by new technology. We get distracted by the pursuit of money. We get distracted by what others think, especially team members or customers. It's too easy for our own thoughts about what we stand for to be drowned out by immediate priorities. That's when it's time to ask some tough questions. *Do I want to be known for my integrity? Do I want to be known for being understanding? Do I want to be known for being empathetic, curious, and focused? Do I want to be known as someone who gets things done and always delivers top sales? Do I want to be all of these and more?*

No matter their role, great retail leaders start by letting everyone know what they stand for.

When you decide what you want to stand for, your focus will tighten. You will have something firm and clear to aim at. It will become easier to ignore the noise and zero in on the things that matter. And people will know how to describe you.

As a senior leader for many years, I have always stood for clear communication. I'm committed to sharing information that invites everyone on the team to understand the overall direction of the business and recognize their part in the bigger picture. I strive to let everyone see how their day-to-day work helps them achieve their goals. And I consistently make an effort to explain the why behind business decisions and communicate how the choices I make can impact my team members' lives.

What do you stand for?

HOW TO PUT IT TO WORK

Hold a daily or weekly all-hands meeting: The daily meeting (the chat-in, the daily download, the morning meeting, whatever you want to call it) was born in stores. The only way you can ensure that everyone knows what you stand for is to talk about it...all the time!

When I host a morning meeting, I share a transparent view of the sales results and the behaviors demonstrated to achieve them. It doesn't matter if a team member is attending their first morning meeting or have been with the company for years. They walk away with the same outcomes: an understanding of business priorities, an overview of recent progress against key metrics, and likely a real-time view of the team contributions and performance. And maybe have some fun!

When you hold transparent and honest daily or weekly meetings, you set the tone for your store or company. By openly sharing valuable information, you encourage others to do the same. For everyone on the team, these meetings are an opportunity to understand the business and make the team know what you stand for.

Stay connected: While a daily or weekly all-hands meeting is a great start, it doesn't go all the way. A messaging platform such as a group text, WhatsApp group, or Slack channel gives everyone a way to share information and learn from each other. In addition to contributing to a culture of transparency, it helps build the perception of a store or company that functions as a team, even when not everyone is present.

When you encourage people to stay connected, you create a way to share new ideas and have conversations about better ways to run the business. Are the right groups speaking to each other? And how often? By promoting team members' means to have a voice, you can maintain a culture of transparency and receive meaningful feedback quickly.

Apologize when necessary: No matter the circumstances, it's always good to apologize when you're in the wrong, even for seemingly minor issues. This sends the message that you respect other people and care about their feelings. Let it be a part of what you stand for.

PATRICIA ELMALEH
General Manager, thirty years in retail

"I look for someone with a vision, who is not afraid to fight for their people, who leads by example, who walks the walk, who inspires others, is transparent, and ultimately always develops more leaders."

ORLANDO ROBLE
Assistant Store Director, ten years in retail

"Great leaders build a framework for decision-making that includes: your ideals, how you want to be perceived by others, your intentions, and your strengths. Then tell everyone around you about it."

BE KNOWN AS SOMEONE WHO GETS THINGS DONE

What do people think of you at work?

I don't know about you, but that question makes me feel a little insecure. I might say, *"I don't know, they think well of me...I hope?"*

We have all met someone who is always busy but rarely achieves their goals. It's easy to find people in every store/company rushing around from one idea to the next, often working overtime to generate more work for themselves and other people, but rarely taking the actions needed to finish a project.

That's why this is one of the foundations of great retail leadership: be known as someone who gets things done!

People who get things done are driven by an insatiable desire to make progress and help others.

People who know how to get things done can be analytical and intuitive, aggressive or patient as required, and confident and humble at the same time. They instinctively know when and how to escalate issues to the right level without being asked to do so. They have a unique ability to cut through the confusion, get straight to the problem, and negotiate compromises to get better and likely faster results.

People who get things done are driven by an insatiable desire to make progress and help others. They are not looking to build a cache of favors or special attention and are unwilling to make deals that compromise the solutions that can come back to haunt them.

Of course, you can't control how other people think about you. But there are a few simple things you can do to build a strong reputation for action. You just need to demonstrate to others that you are consistently in it to win it. Everyone likes being around people like that!

Here are a few more ways you can develop an excellent reputation for getting things done.

MY REPUTATION FOR "GOING GREEN"

Color is a powerful tool. For centuries, color has been used to influence human behavior because of its ability to inspire different emotions. While the feeling that color evokes is different for each person and unique across life experiences, *there is one color that always brings me joy. Green.*

Green is the color of hope, growth, and rejuvenation. It is the color of life and sustainability. It's the color of my birthstone, the emerald, known to give intuition and abundance to those who wear it. Sometimes green represents greed or envy, but generally speaking, it is a welcoming color, and for me, a *winning* one.

> People who get things done are not looking to build a cache of favors or special attention and are unwilling to make deals that compromise the solutions that can come back to haunt them.

For many years, and for several different companies, I have attached my name to a concept that I call *"Going Green."* It started as a straightforward concept, indicating that you were "green" when your results were positive against a goal, yellow when there was a slight miss, and red if the results were significantly off target. The concept of *"Going Green"* could refer to any key performance indicator: sales against last year's, units per transaction, Net Promoter scores, conversion, or any other relevant metric.

Over the years, however, the concept has taken on a life of its own and developed in numerous unexpected ways. For a national conference, I invited an entire region of stores to dub themselves the Green Hornets and organized custom spray-painted shirts, with a green hornet motif, for a hundred leaders. I've seen stockrooms being painted green, witnessed green dollar signs hanging from the ceiling like stars in the sky, and smiled as leaders have chosen to wear green to meetings to show their commitment to great results.

The examples above are the tip of the iceberg. I would say green is my signature color. I put my name to the concept of *Going Green*, almost as I'd put my name to a trademark. If you are reading this book and have worked with me, you will be smiling right now because you know it's true. *Going Green* enshrines the assumption that results will be more positive than negative, more green than red. It is a way of conveying my pride in my retail career and putting my name to a concept I believe in.

I'm proud of having the color green attached to my name; it's one of the ways I have developed a reputation for getting things done.

How will you define success in your career? If you want an excellent one, you need to go further than just doing a good job. You must be the best you can be—alert, lively, enthusiastic, knowledgeable, learning from others, and generous in sharing what you know.

HOW TO PUT IT TO WORK

Show up on time: I believe that if you consistently show up late, people will think you're flighty and don't know what you're doing. I have found that building a reputation for excellent work starts with just being five minutes early to everything. It's that simple.

Take control of your own career development: Career development is a responsibility shared between you, your leader, and your company. The company may offer the tools and feedback to help you prepare yourself, and your leader may provide great insight on how to get there, but ultimately, it's up to you to promote you. And team members who work on themselves, set goals, and take control of their own development are people with strong reputations. Companies want to invest in people who invest in themselves.

Manage your time: One of the best habits you can develop to build an excellent reputation for getting things done—in business and in life—is effective time management. We all have the same amount of time in a day. However, not everyone uses their time effectively. The trick is to ensure that you're putting your attention toward the things that will help you move forward the fastest, not frittering away precious minutes and hours engaging with time wasters.

Demonstrate great attention to detail: Small gestures—like a handwritten thank you note to a colleague or sticking around late to make sure everything is perfect for the next day's business, will strengthen your professional reputation as someone who recognizes and pays attention to the details. Just doing what's expected isn't enough to improve how others see you. You want to stand out!

Make other people look good: Another way to add weight to your positive reputation is by going the extra mile to help your team. That could be by offering an extra hand when you know they're inundated with tasks or making them look great in a meeting. However you do it, helping out those around you can be extremely rewarding, both personally and professionally.

HIRE THE RIGHT PEOPLE

Every great retail leader knows this, but it's worth repeating here: you can have the best strategy in the world, incredible product to sell, and the most compelling vision

GAIL TOPAL
Regional Vice President, forty years in retail

"I'm proud of my reputation and the success of the people who have worked for me. When someone stops me as I walk down the street to share a great story of how I made a difference in their career, it makes me very proud."

LEANDRA REID
Twenty years in retail

"During my twenties, I held an executive assistant position, and the leadership team appreciated my consistent performance, entrepreneurial attitude, and how I inspired the team through my commitment to helping others. I had some high school retail experience on my resume, so the VP asked me to help his wife open a retail store. Twenty years later, I co-founded Vetrina Group, which exists to support retailers in their expansions!"

KRISTIN SMITH
Store Manager, twenty-nine years in retail

"Be the hardest worker in the room and never underestimate the power of your words. Your people are watching every move you make, so lead by example every second."

for what you want to achieve, but it's all wasted if you don't have the right people in place. Walt Disney put it this way: "you can dream, design, create, and build the most wonderful place in the world, but it requires people to make it a reality."

> You can have the best strategy in the world, incredible product to sell, and the most compelling vision for what you want to achieve, but it's all wasted if you don't have the right people in place.

We know that today's customers are savvier and more informed than ever. They can shop from anywhere, including the comfort of their home, and the product choices available to them in every category are almost unlimited. In an environment of incredible opportunity, how will you differentiate your business?

Simply put, you can't afford to undervalue the importance of anyone on your team. Your people are a critical differentiating factor. Whether by providing incredible training, offering unique benefits, or creating a winning culture, you need to find ways to attract and keep team members with the people skills and service-oriented attitude today's customers expect.

But remember that customer experience can mean different things to different people. As you build this incredible team, consider the complementary skill-sets of individual team members. For the best results, a great retail team should represent a wide variety of skills. This enables the team to attract and retain all customers, build better rapport with them, and blow their socks off!

Ask any hiring manager or recruiter, and they will tell you that there is no universal formula for finding the ideal employee or building the typical complementary team.

Every role is different, every company has different expectations, every brand has a unique culture, and very few candidates excel in every aspect of a position. But when it all works, magic happens!

HOW TO PUT IT TO WORK

Don't miss the yellow flags: We all understand the concept of red flags. If you've hired a lot of people, you can probably list the red flags you might find on a resume: spending too little time at each company, significant unexplained gaps between jobs, and similar issues. Green flags, conversely, indicate that you have found a great candidate. But don't forget the yellow flags. These are places where you need to keep probing. Ask for more examples. Dig a little deeper. Your job is to tease out problems, not gloss over yellow flags because you need to hire someone quickly.

Don't decide by yourself: A time constraint, an open position, and the mindset of "good enough" can cloud your judgment. If you're unsure, don't just pull the trigger. Bring the candidate back in again to meet another member or two of your team. Before they arrive, make sure you are clear on the areas you want your fellow interviewers to probe. The candidate may rise to the occasion, but more often than not, the additional scrutiny will reveal hidden issues and turn a "maybe" into a solid "no."

Don't settle for just okay: Every company wants to hire the best people. You can't succeed without reliable, trustworthy, competent, engaging team members. In some situations, it's tempting to believe that anyone is better than no one. This is particularly true when a position has been unfilled for a while and there's pressure to fill it.

But here's what I know: the cost of a bad hire can far exceed the additional workload of leaving a position vacant. *What are you saying to your team when you hire a candidate who's just okay? That you lower the bar when the going gets tough. That the work you've all put into building a phenomenal team isn't actually that important.* That's without even considering the long-term impact of customers who, after interacting with a mediocre employee, may not return to your store.

Be open to nontraditional work histories: This is one of my favorite principles for building a high-performing store team and a robust culture. Even if a job you're trying to fill has a long list of requirements, that doesn't mean you can't offer the position to someone who comes from a nontraditional background.

Instead of limiting your search to candidates who have all the "right" skills, connect with those who fit your company culture. Look for someone who has that special spark that you know will add value to the team, even if they lack specific relevant experience. Motivational speaker, Zig Ziglar, said it best, "It's your attitude, not your aptitude, that determines your altitude."

Ask behavior-based questions: An interview is a chance to probe a candidate about specific accomplishments listed on their resume, with the intention of understanding how they approach the world. Ask questions that start with, "Tell me about a time when..." Ask what steps the person took to achieve a particular result, what challenges they faced along the way, and what he or she learned. How the candidate responds to this line of questioning will reveal a lot about their character.

Get your team in on the game: Before posting a job to the general public, tap into your company's existing chain of connections, namely your team. While many companies often rely on employee referrals to discover new talent, you may benefit from taking this process a step further and involving your team directly in the recruitment process. Nobody understands what it's like to work in your existing culture—or who will enhance it—better than your current team.

Get out into the community: In your search for the perfect candidate, don't be afraid to tap into local communities. Let's say you're searching for a new assistant manager. Instead of merely posting a listing online, send a member of your team to events leaders typically attend, such as mall meetings,

Meetups, or networking events. Tapping into a specific talent pool can yield excellent results, especially when it allows you to connect with candidates who aren't actively pursuing opportunities.

Use social media: This may sound obvious, but search for individuals with relevant prior experience on LinkedIn or locate Facebook groups that cater to the types of candidates you're seeking. You can even search for keywords associated with the open position's key skills on Twitter and Instagram. Find candidates where they already spend their time...on social media.

RICK PLANOS
Consultant, twenty years in retail

"Hire smart, and don't be afraid to hire people more intelligent than you. They only make your team better. I've been involved with several startups, and building the right team is exponentially more critical because they are the heart of the brand. If the startup catches on and you expand, those first hires will be the foundation of the company leadership."

> **WILLIAM BROBSTON**
> President, The Brobston Group
>
> "Quite simply, the quality of your people will determine your success. Recruit and hire energetic, dedicated, respectful, ambitious, and compassionate leaders. Train them to represent and amplify your brand messages. And work consistently to retain them by providing a path for various kinds of growth."

MAKE EVERYONE FEEL IMPORTANT

Every person is equally essential to the overall function of a team. Period. That's true in any business, but especially in retail. In the retail business model, no one is insignificant. We all need each other. When one piece of the puzzle is missing, it's incomplete.

Whether a team consists of three people in a small family-run boutique or ten thousand connected to a huge company, it can only thrive when everyone does their part and is valued and appreciated, no matter their role. *People will walk through fire for a strong, competent leader who makes them feel important.*

This ideal has been instrumental in my leadership. I believe it's one of the critical factors in my success. As you read in the introduction, I clearly understand where this element of my personality comes from, because I learned it from my grandfather. What do a CEO and a temporary construction worker on a job site have in common? You won't know until you start a conversation, show empathy, be curious, and listen. My grandfather could discover common ground with almost anyone in ten minutes or less, and everyone around him felt important.

> **People will walk through fire for a strong, competent leader who makes them feel important.**

Today's retail workplace requires all of us to pay close attention to everyone in our sphere. We must be active and attentive listeners, practice patience, appreciate others' unique talents and capabilities, and express gratitude for our team's effort and performance. People are carefully observing their leaders, vigilant for reasons not to trust them, but ultimately wanting those leaders to prove themselves worthy of respect and loyalty.

> **Today's retail workplace requires all of us to pay close attention to everyone in our sphere.**

Let's all take a lesson from my grandfather and make everyone around us feel important today by considering doing some of the following things.

HOW TO PUT IT TO WORK

Roll up your sleeves: Great retail leaders roll up their sleeves and get in the mix. And I don't mean simply answering the phone or restocking a shelf. Unload the truck. Process the shipment. You will see things from a different perspective, one you could never get just from conversations with other managers. The view from zero feet reveals every detail about processes and working conditions, opinions about policies, and alignment with company direction. Digging in is an enormous opportunity for connection and discovery.

Be specific with your feedback: One of the best ways to make everyone around you feel important is to be highly specific in your feedback. *"You're awesome to work with"* isn't effective feedback. Neither is *"You did a great job."*

Too often, managers express feedback vaguely, leaving people wondering what they need to do more, better, or differently. Give people a specific, positive direction, and you'll likely find that they respond far better. Rather than saying, *"You need to be more talkative in meetings,"* offer something concrete and positive, founded on your observations. For example: *"You're smart. I want to hear at least one opinion from you in every meeting we're in together going forward."* That's how you make everyone feel important.

Guide people to the source of their own power: My grandfather inspired me to see that there is no greater joy than helping people see a vision for themselves and find their light. *Supporting those around us to reach higher levels than they believed possible is one of the most rewarding responsibilities of leadership.* Offer members of your team support and motivation as they find their own way and demonstrate their capabilities. All you need to do is believe in them and offer guidance when asked.

Be consistent: Among influential, respected leaders, this is key. Be consistent in your expectations of people, so they always understand their roles. Over time, consistently doing what you say you'll do builds trust. Keeping your commitments must be the essence of your behavior, in all relationships, day after day, and year after year.

Don't pick favorites: You mustn't play favorites among your team members. If you show the same level of support to all of your employees, assigning tasks and perks fairly, new team members will soon understand that they're on a level playing field. As a result, they will quickly begin to trust and respect you. *Nothing destroys the belief that everyone is important faster than the perception that a leader plays favorites.*

JILL GRANDE
Senior Director, twenty-one years in retail

"The single best quality that makes an exceptional leader is the ability to act as a multiplier. The best leaders make everyone smarter and use their leadership abilities to enhance the qualities of others. Leaders who look to share their knowledge, encourage risk-taking, and create collaborative environments often build the best cultures. To me, cultures attract top talent. People want to work for people, and when you focus on being a multiplier, you attract the right people."

HAVE A GREAT STORY TO TELL

Everyone has a storyteller inside them, and everyone has a story to tell. You just may not know it yet. The difference between people who seem interesting and those who don't is their ability to turn their experiences into compelling narratives. I wasn't clear on my own story until I wrote this book.

ROY MCCOMBS
Freelance Retail Consultant

"We are managing people, not names on a schedule. We understand that our team is a group of individuals, and the way we manage or lead one person may not be what another person needs. Be agile and flexible and develop a leadership "toolbox" of various styles that you implement when needed—you can't build a house with just a hammer, so one leadership style is not going to make the team."

Of course, some people are more naturally gifted in this area than others. But anyone can learn the craft of storytelling, because like so many other skills, it's a series of behaviors and principles. With attention and consistent practice, you can have people hanging on your every word—at professional networking events, in meetings with your team, and in interviews.

In a results-focused retail environment, storytelling with data is a subtle art that can lend credibility and impact to any argument. Nothing summarizes an issue like an inarguable series of numbers, although that is not usually the most exciting part of the story! In retail, we traditionally track our results daily (even hourly!), week by week, month by month. We plot them against our goals, then seek to understand both the results and the behaviors through which we achieved them.

In a results-focused retail environment, storytelling with data is a subtle art that can lend credibility and impact to any argument.

While metrics are essential, the journey of *how* they are achieved is equally important. As you practice the craft of storytelling, ask, "What were the results I delivered, and how did I achieve them?" This simple question can be your mantra for the rest of your career.

Don't be afraid to accept some of the credit yourself. Everything you do, every result that you deliver, every promotion you earn, every customer compliment you receive, is part of your story as a leader. To those of us working in retail, this attitude can feel strange; we tend to give away credit to everyone else. We serve others so that it's part of our DNA, so we often celebrate the team before we honor ourselves.

HOW TO PUT IT TO WORK

What does the audience need to know? A compelling story requires emotion. But every story is really just a sequence of events told in the right order. Extraneous information slows a story down and makes people wonder what the point is.

So how do you know what's essential to tell while captivating at the same time?

You need to tee up the concepts before you start to tell it. Why were you in the situation that you were in? What context does the audience need to appreciate the rest of the story? This shouldn't be every detail of your life, but you should succinctly explain how you got into the situation you're about to discuss.

Once you've done that, think about the logical order of events. This is often—but not always— the chronological order. For emotional effect, you can throw in some small details that aren't totally relevant to the story, but don't get bogged down in extraneous information.

Don't shy away from your emotions: Two people can talk about the exact same experience with wildly different results. One captivates, while the other has members of the audience checking their watches. We tend to appreciate the exciting stories, but the difference between a good story and a bad one isn't the subject matter. It's the emotion the storyteller infuses into their narrative.

Every story has an emotional core, and it comes from the storyteller's feelings about the events they're describing. Think about how you felt when the experience took place. What was motivating for you? What troubled you? How did you feel about your surroundings? If you can express that, you can connect with your listeners, and they'll hang on every word.

As I was writing this book and telling my own story, the balance between facts and feelings was essential. The results I delivered in my career were directly influenced by the emotional core I developed very early. I have often referenced my grandfather as that source of inspiration. It's a big part of my story, and I have learned not to shy away from it.

While I encourage you to track your statistical success and share it as part of your story, you don't need to measure everything, all the time. You make the decision on what's essential to articulate your journey. Is it sales volume growth, performance to budget, or conversion? It all depends on the story you want to tell—just make it a great one!

Tell your story to everyone who needs to know it: It's vital that you communicate your key performance indicators and behavioral metrics in all directions: up, down, and sideways. Your leader wants to know what's going on, and so does your team. They won't be motivated to improve unless they know how they're doing. Most of the suggestions on how to improve will come from your team anyway!

JENNY AGUON
Homeschooler, thirteen years in retail

"Not every metric will be achieved, but progress is sometimes the biggest indicator of success. Don't get stuck in endless accountabilities, goals, forms, and so on. Stick to what speaks to the company's mission and overall goal. Retail is a constant roller coaster. Right when you are going down, you will quickly go back up. Just take it one day at a time."

LEANDRA REID
Retailer for twenty years

"An exceptional retail leader integrates bottom-up logic with top-down strategy, incorporating all necessary data to make the right decisions."

LET'S WRAP IT UP

When I was a store manager at Apple in 2008, our assistant manager, Steve Hawkins, introduced the concept of the flywheel to our team. A flywheel is *"a mechanical device specifically designed to efficiently store rotational energy. The amount of energy stored in a flywheel is proportional to the square of its rotational speed and its mass."*

Why is this important? Every day, in a store where customers waited in line for hours to buy this new thing called an iPhone, we did our best, but it certainly wasn't easy. As we struggled to find our footing and left exhausted every day, the flywheel resisted speed. After a rocky start, however, in about ninety days, we started to deliver record-breaking results by changing some of the team, creating processes to ensure an exceptional experience, and dedicating ourselves to a new way to work. We won international awards for service. The team was thriving, and career growth began. The flywheel had begun to turn, and the energy stored in it created magic.

The process resembles relentlessly pushing a giant, heavy flywheel, turn upon turn, building momentum until a pivotal point and beyond.

I didn't know it at the time, but the flywheel effect is a concept developed in the 2001 book *Good to Great* by Jim Collins. No matter how dramatic the result, good-to-great transformations never happen overnight. There is no single defining action, no grand program, no killer innovation, no solitary lucky break, no miracle moment. *Instead, the process resembles relentlessly pushing a giant, heavy flywheel, turn upon turn, building momentum until a pivotal point and beyond.* Steve knew this and pushed us to spin the flywheel every day.

When I reflect on why we had this breakthrough to success that year, here is what I recall:

- There was an incredibly optimistic attitude from everyone on the team about what we wanted to accomplish; nothing was going to stop us.
- We told everyone what we stood for, both as a brand and as a store leadership team.
- We wanted to get that flywheel moving, and we were going to be known as the team that got things done.
- We hired the right people and never lowered our expectations.
- We made everyone feel important, celebrated our success and failure together as a team, and created an environment where everyone contributed.

Being a good leader turns the flywheel. Being a good leader helps you drive your team toward greatness. Being a good leader helps you gain professional recognition and visibility beyond your current company, in a way that can inspire your next career opportunity. That's the flywheel at work.

I hope the simple principles described in this chapter will guide your progress. Keep looking for ideas and people who inspire you. Thank you, Steve, for inspiring me and teaching me that the flywheel is real and there is power in spinning it every day.

STEVE HAWKINS
Team Leader, sixteen years in retail

"In everything I did, the concept of 'servant leadership' was what I tried to emulate. People forget about the lunch you bought them in a few days. People will remember you taking care of them forever."

THE SINGLE
MOST PRECIOUS
RESOURCE FOR
ANY GROWING
ORGANIZATION
IS TALENTED
PEOPLE
SUPPORTED
BY A UNIQUE
AND ENGAGING
COMPANY
CULTURE.

CHAPTER 7

CREATE A WINNING CULTURE

Now let's get to one of my favorite topics in retail leadership—*creating a winning culture!*

When you think about building a team whose members are engaged, motivated, and excited to stick around, there's likely one word you've heard repeatedly: *culture.* And for an excellent reason. The vibe of your store/company and the people who work there every day has a significant impact on your happiness, your results, your reputation, and your overall success.

Let's start by recognizing that everyone describes culture differently, including what it means to them, their experience, and how the role plays in the workplace.

Culture is the personality of a store or company. It's fluid and changes with every new employee.

While I propose culture as the "fun" part of leadership basics, make no mistake: there is a direct correlation between culture and results. One cannot exist without the other. *The best leaders understand that the single most precious resource for any growing organization, regardless of size and industry, is talented people supported by a unique and engaging company culture.*

No doubt, you've heard plenty of praise for the company cultures of giants like Google, Netflix, and Apple. But let's get real: small businesses and smaller corporate retail store fleets can't emulate these examples. You probably don't have access to abundant human resources, huge marketing budgets, brand recognition, or perks like free snacks, ping-pong tables, and daycare.

Every person at any company of any size can play a part in creating a winning culture.

The good news is that you don't need those things to be successful! They may excite new hires, or attract a lot of candidates to work there, but ultimately people want to know where the company is going and why they're working so hard, *and that starts with you.*

Fortunately, we all have the power to influence company culture. We just need to know where to start! Before you skim through the following thinking it doesn't apply to you, *I want to emphasize that every person at any company of any size can play a part in creating a winning culture.*

Let's start by considering the two most common questions candidates ask me during interviews:

- "What is the culture like here?"
- "What are the opportunities for growth?"

These seem quite reasonable, simple questions, because:

- We all want to be in an environment that we enjoy
- Most people want to grow their careers

Perhaps you're now realizing that you may have asked a hiring manager these questions at some point in your career. Here's the hard truth, however: there are no answers to these two questions. *The only person who controls both the company culture and your career growth opportunities is you.*

A better question might be, *"What impact can I have on the company culture here?"* In a small company, individual employees, from the president to sales associates, have a more significant proportional impact on the over-all culture of a company. In a company of ten employees, a single worker makes up 10 percent of the workforce. In larger organizations, you can still exert a significant positive influence; you just have to know where to start.

In the next part of the chapter, I'll share my four primary "culture tips" to develop your strategy for digging in and finding ways to make a positive impact, regardless of your position at your company. *The next time you have a job interview, you won't need to ask what the culture is like. You will be able to say, "Here's how I would make a positive impact on the company culture."*

FIRST, ESTABLISH A SENSE OF BELONGING

Before we can create a winning culture, we have to discuss belonging and the impact it can have on our career experience. Culture will never grow if we feel like we don't belong on the team. People are often linked together by nothing more substantial than the fact that they all work at the same place or in the same store. As a leader, you have the power to change that.

Belonging starts when you generate a deep sense of shared mission and purpose, so that you and your team members know you share the same values and are working toward the same goals. In retail, that always begins with how we choose to serve others.

Belonging is a shared experience, and the strategy for creating it should involve a variety of people on the team. Bringing people together and agreeing on a mission and purpose will also positively impact motivation, health, and happiness. When you feel a connection to others through belonging, you can support each other through both good and tough times.

Belonging starts when you generate a deep sense of shared mission and purpose.

Successful leaders know the importance of creating a strong shared vision. A compelling purpose will also support the great conversations needed to turn goals into reality, so that everyone anticipates an exciting future of success together. *An inspiring vision, rooted in belonging and communicated confidently to the team, provides a rallying cry that energizes everyone to accomplish big things!*

HOW TO PUT IT TO WORK

Start by asking everyone to dream big: Your team wants to feel like they and their work matter. If you help them achieve their goals and find belonging, they will work hard to honor the trust you place in them. Talk to each team member about their dreams and career aspirations, how they see the store/company environment and how they can contribute to making it successful. Imagine the possibilities and ask them to consider these questions:

- What would it look like if we were to do our very best every day?
- What would we like to be known for? This is one of my favorites for any individual conversation or team.
- What accomplishments would we be most proud of?
- What will it take for us to get there? What do we need?
- What's the most important way you, as a team member, can help us get there?

Develop a sense of belonging through a customer-centric purpose: In a healthy culture, people serve a vision bigger than themselves. In the retail business, it's essential to always keep in mind the experience you want your customers to have and communicate it intentionally and consistently.

Here are three simple guiding principles to use as a filter in developing belonging and customer-centricity:

- Stores/companies that are committed to customer-centricity are *passionate,* and honestly believe the customer comes first. They know that without the customer, they cannot succeed in business. They want to see the world through the customer's eyes.
- Stores/companies that are committed to customer-centricity focus on *what the customer wants* and needs and develop products and services accordingly.
- Stores/companies committed to customer-centricity concentrate on *building relationships* designed to enhance the customer's product and service experience.

Imagine that it's five years from now: Your team has had a significant positive impact on the company's results and is being recognized for the best performance in years. Now, ask your team to describe:

- Are we clear on our purpose and values?
- What is the most critical work we are doing?
- How do our customers perceive us?

- How do people feel about working on this team?
- What is the senior leadership of the company saying about us?

When team members imagine exceptional results, whatever success looks like to them, they will likely understand what leads to those results. Incredible things can happen when people discover their purpose, link it to the values of their team and/or that of the company, and create a vision for how they will fulfill it. Sometimes you just need to dream big.

Establish belonging by finding opportunities to volunteer in the community together: Sometimes finding belonging at work is not about the day-to-day business. Great companies make commitments to the bigger world around them, often by volunteering or serving on committees to help others. Volunteering gives you the chance to positively impact the people and community around you. Even helping out with the smallest tasks can make a real difference to the lives of people, animals, and organizations in need.

I joined the Board of Directors of Goodwill NY/NJ in 2019. Their mission aligns closely to what I believe: that our primary responsibility as leaders is eliminating barriers to employment. My contributions in teaching them how to run a great fleet of retail stores has helped increase their revenue and, therefore, helped get people to work. Share your involvement in activities like this to illustrate how you value being part of the community. Encourage your audience to join you in the effort.

NEXT, SET BIGGER GOALS

Once you have defined your purpose and values and established a sense of belonging, the next step is goal setting. *Positive company culture can be incredibly motivating, and your individual, store, and company goals must be big enough to generate excitement.* Take a look at your current goals. Are there any that really stretch you? It's human nature to stay in your comfort zone and create goals that you know you can achieve, but why would you settle for that?

> **Positive company culture can be incredibly motivating, and your individual, store, and company goals must be big enough to generate excitement.**

Have you ever wondered how much you would improve if you swung for the fences? What would happen if, in all seriousness, you doubled, tripled, or even multiplied by ten the targets you set for yourself and your team? These goals need to be challenging but not unattainable, encouraging the team to draw on their best selves. This is how you can achieve everything envisioned in the "imagine it's five years from now" exercise in the prior section.

When we begin to set goals that are outside our comfort zone, a few things happen. I will use my own personal journey of writing this book as an example of setting a big goal:

- We start to *think differently.* Instead of repeating our standard thought patterns, the ones that are too easy, we get serious in every aspect of our life that affects our goals. We know that what we were doing previously won't get us to our new, bigger goals.
  - In the summer of 2019, when I decided that I wanted to write this book, I started thinking differently about how to achieve my goal. For months, I took writing classes every Monday night after work. I found the best publisher for this type of book through recommendations, exploratory calls, and research. Most importantly, I dreamed big that it could really happen.

- This realization inspires us to act differently. Big goals demand that we change our behavior. They require us to learn new skills. We may need to adapt our circle of friends so that we're around people who support us while we make progress toward our objectives.

  - The next step toward writing this book was to *act differently*, change my routine, and find a group of people to support me and hold me accountable. In October 2019, I attended a weekend-long immersive authors' workshop, where I got serious about the content. During this weekend, I met a group of other future authors, all of whom were incredibly impressive and had great stories to tell. This new group of friends, all of us on a similar path, has been the exact new circle I needed to achieve my goal.

- When we work toward bigger goals, we will *do more and become better*. Even if we fail to achieve our giant stretch goals, the shift in mindset will lead to improved performance and make our standard goals much more accessible.

  - The journey to complete this book required me to do more and become better. For example, I changed my morning routine so that I could sit quietly at the kitchen table every morning at 6 a.m. and write before I went to work. I asked for feedback, shared ideas, and became more focused. A year later, in the summer of 2020, as I finish writing, I can confidently say that, although setting big goals can feel overwhelming at times, thinking differently, acting differently, and doing a little more than usual has given me the platform to celebrate our retail pride! Nothing I've done this year has been more rewarding.

Now imagine an entire team of people setting and pursuing bigger goals, while simultaneously offering one another support. What could that team achieve? How big could they dream?

I wrote this book as a big personal goal while simultaneously leading a retail fleet of stores toward their best results in years. Whatever your goals, achieve them by thinking differently, acting differently, and doing more to become better.

HOW TO PUT IT TO WORK

Achieve bigger goals through daily work:
Goals can be simple milestones you set every single day and consistently work toward. For

example, you might intend to sell a million dollars' worth of product over a year. That sounds intimidating, but breaking it down into small daily bites will make it feel less scary. Smaller, achievable goals that lead to something bigger keep you feeling positive and motivated.

Encourage everyone to participate:
Everyone on the team must have the autonomy to create personal goals under the auspices of the team umbrella. Their contributions are critical when setting big goals for the store/ company because it takes everyone playing the game to win. Each person can then spearhead initiatives relevant to their role that will support higher team objectives. Here are a few questions to help start the conversation on setting bigger individual goals:

- What do you enjoy doing? What are you good at, and what type of work is essential to you?
- What would your career look like if you had the power to make it any way you wanted?
- Imagine yourself in the future. You have achieved great career success. What have you accomplished? What does your life look like?
- Where would you like to be in your career in five years? In ten years? In fifteen years?

Help each other get there: No matter your role on the team, it's your responsibility to support everyone around you to help them achieve their goals. There are several ways you can do this:

- Hold regular one-on-ones to find out how things are going for each member of your team.
- Show your team that you're open to questions and offering guidance.
- Support people by giving them advice on how to achieve their initiatives.
- Help your team define milestones or benchmarks as they work toward group and individual goals.

THEN, ASK YOUR TEAM WHAT'S WORKING (AND WHAT'S NOT)

Customer and employee expectations are higher than ever, and word of mouth travels fast! As customers become ever more empowered, culture becomes increasingly essential to results. And your team can tell you exactly what's working and what isn't.

Outside of actual sales numbers, which are quite easy to track, the most valuable statistics measure how well companies are attracting and engaging the best talent in the industry. Vendors can measure "employee pride" using engagement surveys, employee referral rates, voluntary turnover rates, and employee ratings on review sites. These measures can help you understand whether your employee experience is on the right track.

> **The most valuable statistics measure how well companies are attracting and engaging the best talent in the industry.**

Here's an example of a question you might include in an employee survey: *"What is the most important thing your manager or company currently does that enables you to produce great work?"* Respondents can *answer* in their own words. It's up to you to assess their feedback and decide whether you want to continue on the same path or pivot to a new strategy.

Now, not everything is easy to measure. How do you know if your strategies are working in realms that can't be easily understood via surveys and metrics? The answer may sound simplistic, but it's often overlooked: bring some of the team together and talk about your strategies! You need to know what engages your team, what makes them want to stay, what might make them want to leave, and what's important to them. Nothing can replace honest conversations in a safe and trusting environment.

In my working life, I call these conversations *"Ron's Roundtables."* When I visit a store, I give everyone on the team the chance to sign up for a casual conver-

There is no replacement for curiosity.

sation. The format brings me together with a small group of team members, often outside the store where I can ask questions and receive honest answers. No other managers are present. *If I am responsible for making decisions about culture, values, and goals, I want to know what people think. There is no replacement for curiosity.*

Some of the common questions I ask are:

- What would you tell a friend about your store if he/she was about to start working here?
- What would you most like to change about this store/company?
- Who is a hero around here? Why?
- What prevents someone from doing well in the store?
- Do you feel successful every day? If not, why not?

Pay particular attention to what motivates the team and what they care about the most, along with *their* perceptions of the company's strengths and weaknesses. These insights can help you understand both the immediate and long-term steps you may need to take to shift your company culture from where it is today to where you want it to be—collaborative, supportive, participative, and productive.

HOW TO PUT IT TO WORK

Know the score: An essential part of creating a winning culture is understanding what's working. In retail, we do that really well. Tracking progress toward goals also helps teams stay motivated as they see movement and celebrate milestones.

The more you measure, the better you can understand what to do to advance toward your goals. You can use this information about results to motivate your team toward greatness and create a sense of togetherness.

Programs don't replace human interaction: It's easy to confuse things like sales results, the physical store environment, how people dress, punctuality, and the amount of creativity put into stockroom bulletin boards, with the quality of a team's culture.

Without a conversation about how everyone really feels, team members may think the company sees them as something that needs to be "fixed" when a new program is introduced. They may feel their point of view has not been heard. This naturally leads to resistance and cynicism.

Culture is established through honest, thoughtful, trusting conversations. Those conversations, whether it's a "Ron's Roundtable" meeting, an opportunity to touch base one-on-one, a store meeting, or a group outing, can lead you to a deeper understanding of how those around you are feeling, and what you can do next.

FINALLY, ALWAYS RECOGNIZE THE GREATNESS AROUND YOU

Who doesn't like to be recognized for a job well done? We certainly do in retail! We naturally celebrate hard work and sales results. We grew up doing this—it's part of our pride.

Employee recognition has long been a cornerstone of effective leadership. But today, as the competition for talent escalates, valuing teams and recognizing greatness is more critical than ever.

An excellent recognition program can be part of this process. If you don't have one, create one! Everyone wants to know how they are doing, and a formal program can build momentum toward big goals. *Each time you reward or recognize the greatness around you, you show your team which values and behaviors you want to celebrate.*

When it comes to always recognizing greatness, here are the basics:

> **Each time you reward or recognize the greatness around you, you show your team which values and behaviors you want to celebrate.**

- **Be specific, be relevant:** Recognition is more meaningful when tied to a particular accomplishment or business objective. When recognizing the team, explain what the honor is for. This will help them connect what you are celebrating to the behavior you are describing.

- **Be timely:** Recognition that arrives months after success isn't nearly as meaningful as immediate recognition. The longer it takes for you to recognize greatness, the less authentic your affirmations will seem to employees. Make employee recognition a priority and have formal systems in place so you never miss a deadline.

- **Remember, it can come in many forms:** There is a great deal of research that indicates people are motivated by more than money. Everyone has their own preference or style when it comes to giving and receiving appreciation. Some prefer it to be public, others prefer it to be more private. Ask them.

- **Look out for the little things:** While it's crucial to recognize significant accomplishments, everyday appreciation can motivate employees just as much, sometimes even more. I send a lot of handwritten notes and use conference/video calls to celebrate great behaviors or results. These forms of recognition can come from peers or managers. For some employees, appreciation from peers may be even more motivating than praise from managers.

- **Connect to the bigger picture:** Recognition helps team members see that their manager values their contribution to the success of the team and company. It helps employees feel secure about their value to the company, motivating them to continually deliver great work. Regularly share news about the company's progress toward specific goals and explain how individual employee successes relate to the larger vision.

Once you have established belonging, set bigger goals, and confirm that the strategies you have implemented are working. Celebrating the greatness around you is the fun part!

HOW TO PUT IT TO WORK

Understand the importance of the *how*: *what* your team members achieve can be less important than *how* they achieve it. There are two different ways to think about this:

- **Incentives that center on the "what:"** Focus your efforts here if sales or other key performance indicators are the most critical aspects of your culture. Specific incentives for maximizing sales can push your team to reach new heights!
- **Incentives that center on the "how:"** These are programs that revolve around the *behaviors* exhibited on the path to reaching desired results. They allow you to reward your team for taking specific actions aligned with you/your company's core values. This sends a signal to other team members about the behaviors you value.
- **Both are important:** Consider the pros and cons of individual rewards versus collaborative

team rewards. No one plan will work for every store/company. Take into consideration what your team values and what you need to achieve, and always filter initiatives through an understanding of the culture you're looking to support.

LET'S WRAP IT UP

I hope I've convinced you that a winning culture is an indispensable element of business success, and that I've given you some practical tools you can use to build one. Whatever position you hold, the more quickly you can make an impact when you start in a new role, the more attention and support you will receive. Remember to measure your results so that you can share what you did and have a story to tell.

The evolution of a great culture requires considerable time and effort. And honestly, no culture is perfect.

That said, building culture is a slow, deliberate process. You can't simply scatter seeds and expect fruit and flowers to spring up overnight. Create formal initiatives, suggest better ways of doing things, and focus on giving your best every time you walk through the door.

The evolution of a great culture requires considerable time and effort. And honestly, no culture is perfect. But you can always be working on incremental improvement and enjoying the ride and the results that come with it.

PART IV

WHAT'S NEXT?

NO MATTER
WHERE WE
ARE IN OUR
JOURNEY,
PART OF
"WHAT'S
NEXT" IS
THE MOVE
TOWARD
INTENTIONAL
LEADERSHIP.

CHAPTER 8

FROM ACCIDENTAL TO INTENTIONAL

Many of us are thrust into management positions with little or no preparation. This is undoubtedly true in retail, and I have personally met hundreds of managers who would describe themselves as having an accidental leadership career.

Often, we start by filling in for an open role. When those around us are not sure what to do, we step in and help them figure it out. We begin leading long before we have a title. Eventually we may find ourselves responsible for other needs, filling bigger and bigger gaps, and serving more and more people.

My first multi-store role was as a district manager for GAPKIDS, a role to which I was promoted after a series of "stretch assignments" and a surprise visit from the SVP of stores. I will never forget the fear I felt. I said to myself, "Now what do I do?"

Coming into leadership by accident, we may not even realize what has happened until we look around and see that we have followers, who stick with us as our careers shift and grow. *No matter where we are in our journey, part of "what's next" is the move toward intentional leadership.*

At the beginning of this book, we discussed how many people fall into retail accidentally. I encouraged you to take pride in your career and see it as a source of connection and deep satisfaction. We have also explored my retail leadership basics and pillars of expertise.

The last step on our journey together is to move the conversation from accidental to intentional. Now that you've taken ownership of your retail career, you can be proactive in developing it. This chapter is about giving you the opportunity to thrive for years to come.

Throughout these pages, I've emphasized that *intentional* relationships with each other and the customer are an essential part of a great retail career. *What does it mean to be intentional with your relationships? It means you are purposeful in word and action. It means you live a professional life that you find meaningful and fulfilling. It means you make thoughtful career choices.*

Once you have developed a robust and highly engaged network, don't be surprised if companies regularly contact you because they're searching for candidates with your specific skills and experience. Recruiters and prospective employers often use websites like LinkedIn to make new connections. When they find promising candidates, they may reach out with enticing opportunities.

What does it mean to be intentional with your relationships? It means you are purposeful in word and action.

Let's examine three critical relationship skills that will help you grow your no-longer-accidental career.

YOUR RELATIONSHIP-BUILDING SKILLS WILL GET YOU YOUR NEXT JOB

You're likely aware that networking is one way to find your next great job. But have you considered that it might be the best way to get that job? *Getting a phenomenal opportunity can be as much about who you know as it is about what you know.*

When you put your time into building your professional network, rather than poring through endless listings online and applying randomly, you will gain so much more.

You are better off developing several parallel networks of people willing to help you than you are relying on a single close-knit group. An extensive network expands your access to opportunities, broadens the range of perspectives you welcome into your life, and diminishes the power any one person holds over you.

How do you go about building this type of network? For many people, the idea of "networking" instills a feeling of panic. Not everyone enjoys the prospect of "working a room." The good news is that anyone, even the most introverted of us, can improve our connection skills with a bit of reframing, practice, patience, and persistence.

> **Networking is relationship building. Your network is the result of creating intentional relationships with people you encounter every day, a few times a year, or once at an event.**

If you find that off-the-cuff conversations make you want to run for the door, consider doing a little groundwork ahead of time. Come up with three open-ended or thought-provoking questions to keep conversations moving. With a little prep work, you will feel more confident, and you can have the fluent conversation you imagined.

I like meeting new people, learning about their experiences, hearing their stories, and figuring out whether we can support each other. All of my career growth opportunities have come from referrals, so my open approach to networking has a lot of positive intent behind it. *"Tell me how you ended up in retail?" "What made you choose that company?" "What has your career path been so far?" "Who was the best leader you have worked for and why?"* The list of ways to exercise curiosity is endless.

Think of it this way: ultimately, networking is relationship building. Your network is the result of creating intentional relationships with people you encounter every day, a few times a year, or once at an event. And that is a skill that you will take with you, no matter where you go!

HOW TO PUT IT TO WORK

Create a networking plan: Everyone is busy, so go into conversations with a specific goal. This will allow you to make the most productive use of your time. If both people understand the context of the meeting and prepare to contribute, you will accomplish more.

Creating a plan will also enable you to rapidly build your professional network, engage with like-minded people, advance your professional persona, and enjoy the opportunities that come along the way. How many new connections do you need to make this week? Be specific.

I encourage you to find a friend, peer, or family member who can hold you accountable by checking in with you weekly on your progress on your plan. Be sure to analyze what is and isn't working, and don't be afraid to change your plan, alter the steps you take to reach your goals, or adjust your expectations. Maybe you will discover that you are even better at networking than you think!

Can you do it over email? Instead of meeting in person, could you trade emails to accomplish the same objective? Choosing to email instead of schedule a meeting allows you to manage your response in a way that fits everyone's priorities and schedule. When I am asked to offer advice to leaders, recruiters, and industry experts, sometimes email is the best way to answer quick questions.

Offer to schedule a breakfast meeting:
Breakfast is the most productive meeting time of the day. An 8 a.m. breakfast meeting usually includes a hard stop and doesn't interfere with anyone's morning business agenda.

What gets scheduled gets done: Even networking requires a schedule. If you find it challenging to make time for it, start slow, but don't give up. I generally set a goal to attend at least one event per month. I choose a function to participate in as early as possible and put it on my calendar. I make the most of the events I attend by showing up with lots of energy, plenty of business cards, and a clear intention to have meaningful conversations with several new connections.

WHAT ARE YOU MOST PROUD OF?

DANA PEREZ-ELHAI
Director of Business Development,
twenty-two years in retail

"I am most proud of the relationships I have made and maintained after so many years. It's how I have been able to have a successful recruiting career."

> ### *WHAT ARE YOU MOST PROUD OF?*
>
> **ANTHONY PIERCE**
> Dual Store Manager, thirty-two years in retail
>
> "I have been able to make lifelong connections in retail. While I have worked at many companies, I'm proud that I have been able to work for two retailers twice in my career. I left each to build my skills, but my relationship with the people kept bringing me back."
>
> **WALT HOLBROOK**
> Consultant, fifty-two years in retail
>
> "I have relationships that I have built for over fifty years. The personal satisfaction of seeing my peers, associates, and friends attaining success. The occasional note from a long-lost associate, finally recognizing how hard I worked to ensure their success."

REPUTATION MANAGEMENT IS A REAL THING

What is the first thing you usually do before accepting a new position or meeting a potential candidate to hire? You search online.

And guess what? That's precisely what most people do before they agree to work with you. This means you might be gaining or losing new career or business opportunities without realizing it, because of your online reputation.

Thanks to digital technology, the retail industry has grown larger in our ability to connect with a vast virtual audience, and smaller because the speed at which information is shared about your work has never been faster. This presents opportunities for and risks to your reputation.

Everyone needs to be aware of best practices in digital personal brand management to develop and safeguard their online presence.

However, there is more to developing a positive professional reputation than merely managing your digital presence. *The tried-and-true method of reputation building is to always do your best work, whatever position you're in so that anyone who hears about your efforts hears only positive feedback.*

As discussed in the previous section, it's more important than ever to cultivate personal real-world connections in conjunction with your digital presence. *Building your reputation is a long game, but even in the short term, every new person you connect with will develop an opinion of you.* Over time, the cumulative impact of these encounters will be like money in the bank—positive social capital—for you and your future.

What should you do if your reputation is in question? First, do not ignore it. When an issue hits, launch your own PR campaign. Find allies who will stick up for you even when you aren't there. Seek advice from people you trust, who have a stellar reputation in the company or industry. One word from the right person can immediately silence all criticism.

> The tried-and-true method of reputation building is to always do your best work, whatever position you're in so that anyone who hears about your efforts hears only positive feedback.

As a hiring manager, I have personally seen the impact of poor reputation management. Several years ago, I hired a new store manager for a company I was leading. The candidate had strong relevant work experience and a great personality, and I was confident that they would be an excellent fit.

I announced to the store team that I had hired a new leader and was due to start. All was moving forward as planned until team members found content I ha missed on Twitter. The new leader had posted numerous racially insensitive comments over the past few months and had continued to do so after I made the job offer.

Members of the store team initially shared these comments with their parents, and subsequently, with me, the legal department, and human resources. I terminated the new leader on his first day. When I questioned him about the posts, to confirm that he wasn't suffering from a case of mistaken identity, he answered, *"Yeah, my mom told me I should stop doing that."*

HOW TO PUT IT TO WORK

Think twice before you post: Before hitting "share" or "comment," ask yourself whether your action is aligned with your personal brand. Regardless of your privacy settings, never publish negative comments about coworkers, business associates, or customers.

Remember, social media interactions are real and personal. The friends you speak to online may be the same friends you see at work the n day. What you do or say on social media affe real people, just as your friends' posts can you. Think about the impact of what you share (and how publicly you share it).

Like your resume and cover letter, the content on your social media accounts reflect your attention to detail, and your ability to communicate well. It's easy to whip up and submit a post on Twitter or LinkedIn, but challenge yourself to stop and read it over before publishing it.

Become an authority within your own niche: The ultimate goal for every professional, brand, or business is to become an expert within their niche. While social media continues to grow, with billions of users generating untold numbers of daily updates, becoming a well-known and trusted authority is much easier.

Do you have a particular skill or a positive point of view about retail? Please share it! Do you have images that represent your exceptional visual merchandising skills? Please share them! You are building a reputation for excellent work and simultaneously defining how it's shared.

Say "thank you" more often: There's no need to complicate the process of reputation management. Sometimes, the simplest things make the biggest difference. When someone posts a compliment online, saying thank you is a great way to build a reputation for positivity.

TORI KELLER
Store Manager, six years in retail

"Be curious, take ownership, be good to your people, be there for your clients, and think out of the box to drive your business. That's the kind of reputation I want. Anyone can shop online, so create emotional relationships with your clients, and maintain them as you would maintain any other relationship in your life."

SAIRA SETHI
Luxury Retail Professional, twelve years in retail

"Be the person who inspires you. Take time to listen to your peers, no matter the circumstance. Embody patience, calm, and a nonjudgmental attitude. This is the reputation I want to have."

BUILD A PERSONAL BOARD OF ADVISORS

If you've made it this far in the book, you may have thought a lot about why you love working in retail. You understand that retail may be an accidental career, but you take pride in what you do and are committed to personal development. You're empathetic, curious, focused, and you are developing your skills. No doubt, you know how to deliver results. Great, but what's next?

It's not reasonable to expect your leader, a peer, or your family to provide you with all of the skills you need to succeed. The concept of having a mentor is bantered around a lot in conversation as a key to success. Take it one step further. *As you think about how to grow your career and skills, consider developing a personal board of advisors.* This is an informal group comprising six to eight people who can help with your professional development.

Treat yourself like a company with a high valuation and a team of people around you to guide your progress.

This group can act as a sounding board, provide feedback on your decisions, and participate in unfiltered conversations that you can't have with colleagues or friends. This group of advisors *doesn't* meet as a whole, however. It's up to you how you communicate with them.

Think about it this way: companies, large and small, often enlist a board of directors to guide them, hold them accountable, and help them see things from fresh perspectives. The same principle can apply to your personal board of advisors. *Treat yourself like a company with a high valuation and a team of people around you to guide your progress.*

The best board will consist of people from a mix of professional backgrounds, each willing to provide genuine advice. You don't want advisors who will default to making you feel good about your choices. For example, your board shouldn't consist of members of your immediate family, as they may be too personally invested in specific outcomes to provide impartial guidance.

HOW TO PUT IT TO WORK

Start with your current professional network: No doubt you already know people who advise you in various ways. All it takes to grow those connections into ongoing relationships is a little effort. The more aware someone already is of your work and abilities, the more effectively they can advise you.

Think about the people who you already see as mentors. Can you ask them to be your advisors? Once you've got them on board, let them know that you appreciate their input and will consider it carefully, whether you eventually follow their guidance or not. You can also give them precise feedback following conversations, letting them know how their advice has helped you with a decision or moved you closer to your goal.

Connect with a senior-level leader: Who has reached a level you aspire to reach someday? Maybe it's a district manager, a regional manager, or a director of stores. Perhaps it's someone who has transitioned from stores to a corporate role. Find an advisor outside of your current company, reach out to them on LinkedIn, be clear about your goal of creating a personal board of advisors, and schedule a quick call in which you ask them to join.

When you speak, be curious about them. *What's their story? What are the stepping stones between you and a position like theirs?* Take notes on the path they took to get to where they are.

When you schedule a call with a senior leader, pick one topic and be concise. Often, these are exceptionally busy people. They may only offer you a few minutes at a time, so they'll appreciate your efficiency. This type of person, myself included, is overwhelmed with information. As you navigate conversations with your personal board of advisors, keep things simple, clear, and short to have a significant impact.

Ask for feedback about your professional presence: Are you able to project the confidence required to make difficult decisions and take control of unexpected situations? Can you maintain your poise and composure under stress? Do you convey a sense of unused "bandwidth" and an ability to take on high levels of responsibility? Or do you project a harried, overwhelmed demeanor that makes others think you are maxed out at your current level? Executive presence is hard to define, but it's a critical piece of retail leadership.

Choose people to help you make big decisions: *Once you have decided that retail is no longer an accidental career, how do you decide which companies to work for, when to make a change, and why?* In interviews, you will need to own every choice you have made so far, explaining each move and telling the story of your career. Before you make a big decision, pause to think about how you will justify it in five years, and again in ten years.

Most candidates will never get the chance to explain their logic for changing jobs because a resume that implies job hopping is often overlooked in the initial screening process. Ask a member of your board, *"Would someone I respect understand and agree with my timing for a job change?"* If you can answer *yes,* you are most likely making the right decision.

Having a board of advisors around you to provide an objective opinion on your choices can add an incredible amount of value to your career. Not just for today, but for years to come.

DAMERON "DEE" FOOKS
Store Manager, six years in retail

"'If you feel like you're not doing enough, you're doing it right.' This was the advice I received from my previous manager, advisor, and now good friend, Tyler Kantor, as I began my journey as a new retail manager."

STEVE YACKER
Managing Partner Yacker/Dunn Talent Group, thirty years in retail

"The best part about retail is the cast of characters: from the crazy bosses to the inspiring leaders; from the people you take a chance on to those you mentor for years; from the peers who are the only ones who understand what you are going through to the lifelong friendships."

LET'S WRAP IT UP

Your next move isn't always clear. At any age and any point in your career, you might ask yourself the question with which we opened this part of the book: *"What's next?"*

You may have taken your first retail job out of necessity, but it has evolved into the accidental career you love. Nonetheless, you may not know what your next move is. I encourage you to discover what aspects of this industry will play to your strengths, even if you need to alter your current path. Whatever you do, *commit to it fully.*

> **Whatever you do, commit to it fully.**

Whether you're aiming to work for a specific brand, secure a particular job, or something else, get clear about your goals. This will make the steps you need to take to get there more apparent. And you will surround yourself with people and immerse yourself in situations that move you closer to your goals.

This is all part of why I encourage you to have a personal board of advisors. You may not even recognize what you're good at. Sometimes, one of your advisors will discover it before you do!

WHAT'S NEXT FOR ME?

Whether I'm working with my team, visiting stores, writing, leading cross-functional meetings, or having coffee with other professionals, my week is jam packed. And if you work in stores or lead a group of them, I know yours is too.

No matter how busy I am, whenever possible, I set aside time to build upon the three fundamental concepts I shared in this chapter: growing my network through relationship-building skills, managing my social media presence and reputation, and staying close to my personal board of advisors.

While this may sound overwhelming, I believe these steps are the secrets to discovering what's next for you. You are committed to this career now, and my goal in this book has been to share everything I know that can help you get wherever you want to go. From now on, everything is up to you, including how you use this book. You can take pieces of this book as inspiration, knowledge, and content to share with friends and colleagues, or you can put some of what you've learned away for the future when it's more relevant.

I wish you all the best of luck in everything you do, and I mean that with the utmost sincerity. I wrote this book with a great love for the retail industry and for everyone who has dedicated their lives to it.

Thank you so very much, and I can't wait to hear about your success!

PRIDE COMES WITH THE REALIZATION THAT WE MAKE A DIFFERENCE.

CONCLUSION

Why did I name this book *Retail Pride: The Guide to Celebrating Your Accidental Career?*

One of my primary goals in writing these pages has been to instill pride into the retail conversation. Even if retail is an accidental career for you, I hope you'll join me in taking a moment to celebrate all the hard work that happens every day in our industry.

Pride comes with the realization that we make a difference. I want you to take pride in participating in goals, giving feedback, demonstrating your eye for detail, and contributing to continuous improvement. Take pride in using your voice and exercising your abundance of skill.

Irrespective of your position or years of experience, know that you are a vital link in the retail chain. I want you to celebrate your importance in the larger picture. What you do every day matters. You are crucial to the industry around you. Be proud of that.

I want you to demonstrate positivity at work. Embrace your company's purpose and mission and the hundreds of years of retail that came before you. I want you to contribute to the vision of what retail will become tomorrow. Remember what you have already achieved and dream of what the future holds. You are part of the history—and future—of retail.

I want you to be proud of what you do, of who you are, and of what you accomplish, now and in the future. You are competent and powerful! The images of store teams I see posted on LinkedIn show people who have pride; they show nothing but smiles, chests out, and chins up.

As you finish reading this book, I hope you're excited to work in retail, no matter what job you have today. I also hope you have some concrete ideas about "how to put it to work." If some of the advice in these pages doesn't apply to your current role, keep the book around and pick it up again in a few years. Use this book as a resource for information, a training guide, a motivational tool, or a gift.

And now I want you to pay it forward. Start a conversation about your retail pride that inspires greatness or validates a decision. Ask whoever you inspire to pay it further forward to someone else who, in turn, pays it forward again. Soon we will create a global outpouring of kindness and celebration of our accidental careers.

Does that sound impossible? It doesn't sound impossible to me. Based on all of the conversations I have had about the topics covered in this book, it's not only possible, it's necessary.

Because retail can connect the world, one good deed at a time.

One compliment, to one customer.

One warm gesture to someone on your team in need.

One conversation that demonstrates your empathy and curiosity.

My grandfather told me it's our responsibility to find the light in others and that if we do everything with integrity and pride, our most significant impact will be ahead of us, and we might not even know it.

My greatest wish is that this book has made a positive impact on you. Now, pay it forward.

With love,

ABOUT
THE AUTHOR

Ron Thurston loves retail. And he's proud of it. Ron has led the retail teams for some of America's most prominent brands, inspired thousands of store employees, and traveled relentlessly across the country to sit and listen to what they have to say.

From a part-time sales associate to a vice president of stores, Ron has put in the hard work that a retail career requires. He wrote this book to share what he learned along the way.

Ron is a fourth-generation Californian, but he and his husband now live in Manhattan.